Globalisation and Industrial Sickness

Globalisation and Industrial Sickness

Dr. Alok Sen

AKANSHA PUBLISHING HOUSE
NEW DELHI • GUWAHATI • VISAKHAPATNAM

AKANSHA PUBLISHING HOUSE
4649-B/21, Ansari Road
Daryaganj, New Delhi-110002
Phones: 23268193, 09435116718
Email: ektabooks@yahoo.com
visit us: www.akanshapublishinghouse.com

Globalisation and Industrial Sickness

First Published 2011

ISBN 978-81-8370-275-1

PRINTED IN INDIA

Published by Akansha Publishing House, New Delhi-110002 and printed at Harmain Offset Printers, Delhi.

Contents

Contents

Preface

Industrial sickness is such a phenomenon which adds to the already bizarre state of affairs in the industrial scenario of India. Industrial sickness results in loss of production, reduction in income and employment, thereby leading to myriad socioeconomic problems. In the developing countries like India, especially in the relatively more backward regions of those countries, closure of industrial units due to sickness brings with it the worst kind of ramification in the labour market. Since the economy is already in the quagmire of unemployment, fresh closure of running units further confounds the problem of unemployment. The lay-offs resulting from closures can never be redeployed by the existing market forces.

Tea industry in Barak Valley is presently in the grip of such industrial sickness. This southern-most part of Assam with lush green tea gardens around, hills on the back and the river Barak flowing through the valley is an abode for the people of various faiths, languages and ethnicities. For about one hundred and sixty years tea industry in Barak-valley nourished the economy of the entire region and provided a considerable back-up support in the sustenance and growth of this region. But due to the changes in the attitude of the British entrepreneurs by he turn of nineteenth century , the Indianisation of the tea industry and frequent change of ownership thereafter along with the changing approach of the new captains of industry brought about significant changes in the whole edifice of the tea industry. The industry started gradually sliding and sloping down to industrial stagnation and consequent sickness.

The common causes of industrial sickness generally are geographical location, acute competition, market recession, infrastructural inadequacy and the likes. While there is no question of explaining away the importance of these factors, a proper investigation of the sickness of Barak Valley tea gardens perhaps calls for somewhat closer scrutiny. Operating under essentially identical geo-socio-economic conditions, why are some gardens sick while the rest are not? With no significant change in the ground situations, why have some gardens performing so well even two decades ago gone red now? These are the questions which have drawn me into this study. While I have not made an altogether different study, I have tried to study differently. After a thorough investigation into the causes of sickness of the tea industry of Barak Valley, this study has also examined the feasibility of and justification for revival of the sick gardens taking advantage of the revival benefits. In all humility I hope that the findings of this study will prove relevant to those concerned with the industrial sickness in general, and sickness of tea industry in particular.

In a research work of this type a researcher must depend upon the generosity of others directly or indirectly for up-to-date information and co-operation. I express my deep gratitude to the managements of selected units (tea estates) for their kind cooperation and for providing essential information. I also express my gratitude to the authorities of Indian Tea Association, Silchar; Tea Board of India, Silchar & Calcutta; Cachar Cha Sramik Union, Silchar; Indian Council of Social Science Research, Calcutta and Delhi; National Library, Calcutta; Institute of Economic Growth, New Delhi; Department of Economics and Statistics, Assam for providing me access to various valuable information.

This book is substantially base on the findings of my doctoral dissertation submitted to Assam University, Silchar. In this regard I express my sincere gratitude to my supervisors Prof. P.R. Bhattacharjee and Prof. P. Nayak, who are actually main source of inspiration for undertaking this research work and publishing this book. I received very valuable guidance from them during the course of this study.

Finally, I am grateful to Akansha Publishing House, New Delhi, for agreeing to publish this book.

Alok Sen

List of Tables

1

Introduction

At the macro level, industrial sickness is a concomitant of modern industrial civilisation. Social progress is achieved by the constant revolutionising of the technical forces of production, by new discoveries of processes and products. It is inevitable that outdated technologies and products which no longer have a market must perish. However, at the micro level, at the level of individual industrial units, it is essential that every attempt should be made to revive a sick unit and when it is impossible to do so, liquidation should be resorted to, only when it is wholly unviable. The incidence of closures tend to be high in economies characterised by fierce competition and in industries with a high degree of obsolescence. Developed economies with their well-established social security systems easily take care of displaced workers by such closures. They provide education, housing and health care and social security through doles and pensions. So even when labour is displaced, the social safety ensured that basic needs were taken care of. Developing and specially the over-populated economies with their limited investible resources and relatively limited alternative employment opportunities, however, cannot easily afford their productive assets and labour force turning non-operational. The resultant loss of jobs, production and revenue are not easily recovered and depending upon the number of persons involved may lead to serious consequences. Industrial sickness has therefore, to be handled carefully to see that its adverse impacts are least on workers and society.

Definition

It is believed that 'sickness' is easily noticeable even by laymen. There are however, certain types of sickness which are not apparent to the lay eye and may be deceptively concealed under blooming health. Hence, it does not remain an easy task to define it.

The Small Industries Development Organisation (SIDO) defined a sick unit in the small-scale sector as an industry which is operating at less than 20% of its installed capacity.

In 1972 the State Bank of India's Committee on Rationalisation of Return in respect of SSI advances, classified sick units as those, whose accounts are chronically irregular and sticky.

In 1975, the State Bank of India's study team on SSI advances redefined the sick units as a unit which fails to generate internal surpluses on a continuing basis to meet its current obligations and depends for its survival, on frequent infusion of external funds.

Definition of Sick SSI Unit by Reserve Bank of India in 2002 as:

"An SSI unit should be considered 'Sick' if

a) any of the borrowal accounts of the unit remains substandard for more than six months i.e. principal or interest, in respect of any of its borrowal accounts has remained overdue for a period exceeding one year. The requirement of overdue period exceeding one year will remain unchanged even if the present period for classification of an account as sub-standard, is reduced in due course;

or

b) there is erosion in the net worth due to accumulated cash losses to the extent of 50 per cent of its net worth during the previous accounting year; and

c) the unit has been in commercial production for at least two years.

This would enable banks to take action at an early stage for revival of the units. For the purpose of formulating nursing programme, banks should go by the above definition with immediate effect.

In 1977 a working group constituted by the members of SIDO and National Institute for Small Industries Extension and Training (NISIET) offered a definition to a sick unit in small-scale sector as an industry which did not fulfill minimum standards of productivity and profitability over a reasonable period due to internal shortcomings and/or external factors while other such industries were performing fairly well. This definition means to say that a unit may be considered sick, when it does not perform its primary function such as production, sales, collection of debt dues and repayment of debts, dues in the normal way – for reasons beyond the control of the management.

According to Sick Industrial Companies (Special Provisions) Act, 1985, a sick industrial company means a medium and large (i.e., non-SSI) industrial company (being a company registered for not less than seven years) which has at the end of any financial year accumulated losses equal to or exceeding its entire net worth and has also suffered cash losses in such financial year and the financial year immediately preceding such financial year. Thus, according to the act, a company is identified as sick at the stage when its net worth has been fully eroded by its accumulated losses.

After the enactment of the Sick Industrial Companies (Special Provision) Act (SICA) of 1985, from 1987, three categories of sick units are being reported:

i) sick SSI units;

ii) non-SSI sick units (as defined in SICA, 1985) and

iii) non-SSI weak units (not covered by SICA).

Upto December 1986, the reporting was for large, medium and small sick units. Units availing bank credit limit of Rs. 1 crore and above were termed large and other non-SSI units were termed medium.

The Reserve Bank of India (RBI) has modified the definition of a sick small scale industrial unit in June 1989 as under:

"A small scale industrial unit should be considered sick if it has at the end of any accounting year, accumulated losses equal to or exceeding 50 percent of its peak net worth in the immediately preceding five accounting years."

Weak Units

The definitions mentioned above are based on the symptoms of sickness assumed in an advanced stage nearing the closure of the unit. The detection of sickness at this level leaves little scope and time to initiate revival. That is why in order to start the revival work much earlier, the RBI has classified the special-care-deserving industrial units into 'weak units'. According to RBI: "An industrial undertaking is termed 'weak', if at the end of any accounting year, it has,

(i) accumulated losses equal to or exceeding 50 percent of its peak net worth in the immediately preceding five accounting years;

(ii) a current ratio of less than 1:1 and

(iii) suffered a cash loss in the immediately preceding accounting year".

The detection of sickness in Tea industry or units gives rise to some special problems. Tea plantation industry is actually a combination of large-scale agriculture and manufacturing. While production of raw leaves is agricultural in nature, its processing and subsequent operations represent manufacturing and related economic activities. This endows tea plantation with some features common in all plantation industries. So as the features of the tea industry are not exactly similar to purely manufacturing industries, the Government of India applies some different criteria to detect and define 'sick tea units'. The Central Government, while declaring a 'tea producing unit' as sick takes into account the following factors (Tea Board Manual, 1953):

a) The tea undertaking or, as the case may be the tea unit, has made losses in three out of five years immediately preceding the year in which such opinion is formed; or

b) The average yield of the tea undertaking or as the case may be, the tea unit, during three out of five years immediately preceding the year in which such opinion is formed, has been lower than the district average yield by 25 percent or more; or

c) The person owning the tea undertaking, or as the case may be, the tea unit, have habitually made default in the payment of wages, or Provident Fund dues as they are under an obligation to pay under law for the time being in force; or

d) The tea undertaking or as the case may be, the tea unit is being managed in a manner highly detrimental to the tea industry or to the public interest.

For the purpose of the present study, we have broadly adopted the definition given by the Government of India as quoted in the immediately preceding paragraph.

Incidence of Industrial Sickness

Though due to regular inventions, and competition in the free market economy the most developed countries of the world were not free from the incidence of industrial sickness, during the period 1972-83, the number of bankruptcies per annum increased from around 10000 to more than 25,000 in the United States, from less than 7000 to around 20000 in Japan, and from around 3000 to more than 12000 in the United Kingdom, the 'sick industries' syndrome in India was quite different from that of the developed nations. As against the

Table 1.1
Industrial Sickness in India (1980-85)

Years	*Number of sick units*	*Outstanding bank credit (Rs. in crores)*
1980	24550	1808.66
1981	26758	1025.54
1982	60173	2585.33
1983	80110	3101.29
1984	93282	3638.39
1985	119606	4270.93
1986	147740	4874.49
1987	205378	4599.10
1988	241814	6028.30
1990	220283	6965.76
1991	222933	7897.61
1992	246911	8887.22

Source: Khanka 1995, pp. 20-21.

natural corporate sickness in market economies, it is largely unnatural in India mainly due to malfunctioning. The phenomenon of industrial sickness appears to become alarming in India and the victims are both large and small units. The Table 1.1 brings out this fact.

It is seen from Table 1.1 that industrial sickness in India has continuously been on the increase and has now assumed alarming proportions. The number of all types of sick units has increased tremendously by nine-times to 246911 as at the end of March 1992 from 24550 as at the end of December 1980. The outstanding bank credit against these sick units has increased by more than four times over the same period. At the end of 2001, the number of sick SSIs stood to 249630 which is 7.4 percent of total SSIs. (Economic Survey 2001-02). Though the small-scale industries have been growing constantly over the years, there has been a gradual increase in the incidence of sickness in the small-scale industries. There are a large number of sick units in small-scale industrial sector. The number of SSIs which was 9.60 lakhs in 1981-82 has increased to 33.70 lakhs in 2000-01. This reveals that number of sick SSIs has increased from 25342 in 1981-82 to 249630 in 2000-01. The number of sick units as a percentage to total SSIs was continuously increasing from 1981-82 to 1988-89 but after that it started declining (except in 1991-92 & 1998-99) and finally reached to 7.4 percent in 2000-01. It is good sign for small-scale industries that the number of sick units as a percentage of total SSIs has been decreased to 7.4 percent (in 2000-01) from 14.0 percent (in 1988-89). But if we compare the present position with that of 1981-82, the situation is not appreciable. The number of sick SSIs increased to 2.84 times as compared to 1981-82 and thus presents a worse situation for SSIs.

One of the worst sufferers of 'industrial sickness' is the Barak Valley (erstwhile Cachar) region of India, located at the southern part of Assam and comprising three districts viz., Cachar, Karimganj and Hailakandi.

Barak Valley: The Region

Barak Valley, a geographical territory with lush green tea gardens here and there, hills around and the river Barak flowing through its heart, is an abode of people of various faith and ethnic origins. Barak Valley has an area of 6962 sq. kms and a population of 29,95,769 according to 2001 census. Geographically this district is bounded at the north by United Mikir Hills, North Cachar Hills District and United Khasi-Jaintia Hills, on the east by the state of Manipur, on the south by Mizo Hills district and on the west by Sylhet district of Bangladesh and Tripura. As a region Barak Valley of Assam now consists of three districts of Cachar, Karimganj and Hailakandi. For administrative convenience, Cachar district (erstwhile) was trifurcated and the three districts Cachar, Karimganj and Hailakandi were created. The undivided Cachar is mentioned as Cachar (erstwhile) in the present work. Climate of the valley is marked by excessive humidity. The onset of rains in the valley is generally experienced in the month of April. The temperature is maximum in the month of May (39.6^{0}C) and minimum in January about 6.8^{0}C. The average annual rainfall is 3311.8 mm with reference to year 2007. Composed of hills, low lands and level plains, this valley depicts a heterogeneous landscape. Geographically, this valley consists of four categories of lands–the hills, plains, intermittent high land (locally called *tilla*) and low land area full of water called *bheel* or *haor*. Roughly the land in Barak Valley covers as follows : plateau 20%, *tilla* 30%, plain land 45%, *bheel* 5% (Dept. of Economics & Statistics, Assam). The high lands are planted with tea. The low lands are cultivated with crops like paddy, pulses, oilseeds etc. and the plains are used for residential purposes. The valley has rich and fertile soil on the one hand and fine grained sand stones and shells on the other. The soil contains a large percentage of organic matter and remains fertile due to annual deposition of silt. The suitability of this region for tea cultivation is well established from the quotes of T Fisher* (1934) exploring the possibility of tea plantation in Cachar comparing various aspects with the tea producing regions of China.

> In regard to climate it would appear that neither the heat nor cold are as intense in Cachar as in China but the rainy season would seem to occur at precisely, in the same time in both countries, the rivers in Cachar being swollen from February as in the tea districts.

* Letter from T Fisher, Esq, AAGG, to G S Gordon, Secretary, Committee for Tea Culture, London, dt. 25th March, 1834.

> The conditions of the atmosphere accompanying the blowing of certain winds appears to be precisely similar in both tracts. The latitude of Man-choo-foo one of the tea districts, is the same with that of much of Cachar. The face of the country appears similar, there being both mountains and hills, the bases of which are worked by numerous rivers and lakes flowing through river tracts with gentle falls to the sea. The soil on the slopes near the foot of many of the hills and mountains is such as Dr Abel states of the tea plant to be grown upon; viz., loose and gravelly formed by the debris of sandstone, silts and granite and containing very little vegetable mould.

The importance of tea industry in the economy of Barak Valley can hardly be exaggerated, as this industry constitutes the major part of organised sector in this far-flung corner of the country. Next to agriculture, tea industry is the only labour intensive industry giving employment to large number of people in Barak Valley. In 2001 average number of people employed on daily basis in tea gardens in Barak Valley was 59,501 and about 4,00,000 persons were dependent on tea industry for earning their livelihood. (Indian Tea Association, Silchar Branch).

A major portion of income in this valley is generated from tea industry. This industry is a major contributor to Government exchequer in the form of cess, agricultural income tax, excise duty, sales tax etc. Moreover, the tea industry gives support to many other ancillary industries like cane, bamboo and services like transport, supply etc. Many local cultural, educational, sports and social institutions and welfare activities get financial support from tea gardens.

Tea is a major export earner for India. Tea of Barak Valley constitutes 5 percent of the total tea export of India (Indian Tea Association, Silchar Branch). But the export market of Indian tea is dwindling gradually. The country's position has slipped from that of premier tea producing country of the world to a poor fourth position. In order to regain the lost position and meet the domestic demand (increasing at a rate of 4 percent per annum), the Indian tea industry needs to accelerate its current rate of growth of tea production. Barak Valley tea cuts a sorry figure here; the average growth rate was only

3.8% as on 1994 and during the period 2001 to 2007 the gross production marked a decline showing a annual average rate of -1.8% . Moreover, the land productivity in Barak Valley is the lowest in North east India. About 50 percent of the tea bushes are above the age group of 50 years, re-plantation is about 0.5 percent as against the desired rate of at least 2 percent per annum. The matter of greater concern is the existence of 28 sick tea estates out of 102 estates in Barak Valley constituting 20 percent of the total tea grant area. And another demoralizing fact is that out of the total tea grant area only 39 percent have been utilised so far for growing tea.

The tea industry is ecologically very beneficial to the valley, which often does not get highlighted. The 'green cover' that it provides, helps in conservation of the environment and cooling down the climate.

So, this study, which intends to find out the causes behind the low productivity, stagnation, low rate of re-plantation and sickness in gardens, may play an important role in the effort of revival and development of tea estates in Barak Valley. The suggestions for solving these problems coming out from this study will certainly be helpful to the organisers in making policy decisions.

History of Tea Plantation in Barak Valley

The development of tea industry in India is the legacy of British administration. The British's adventure to develop tea plantation in Assam dates back to 1823. The East India Company which had trading monopoly right in China and India used to import tea into Britain from China right from 1715 onwards(Griffith 1967). The adverse trade balance and the loss of its monopoly of tea trade with China in 1833 necessitated British authority to develop tea plantation in India. The tea plant was first discovered in Assam in 1823 by Robert Bruce, the merchant and soldier of East India Company while he was confined to Rongpur by the Burmese, he learnt from a Sinpho Chief, that the tea bushes existed in natural fashion. His brother Charles Alexender Bruce took initiative to procure tea bushes and tea seeds. He sent few specimens to the director of Botanical Garden, Calcutta who pronounced it as belonging to the same family but not the same species as the Chinese plant. Later, Major Jenkings and Lt. Charlton investigated in this field and proved that the tea shrub was indigenous in Assam. Subsequently, tea nurseries were developed by the Govt. in Upper Assam. The first tea garden was started at Chabua in Dibrugarh district in 1837.

The tea plantation in the Barak Valley (erstwhile Surma Valley during the British period) was taken up after the annexation of Cachar in 1832. For the first time tea gardens in Barak Valley were started in 1855 at Bursangaon and Gungurpar (Griffith 1967). Subsequently it was developed in Kathal, Silcoorie and Arcattipore and in many other places near Silchar. The opening of Assam-Bengal Railway in 1892 facilitated quick transportation of tea to Chittagong and Calcutta. By the first quarter of the 20th century as many as 100 gardens were established in Barak Valley..

2

Tea Industry of Barak Valley: The Pre-Independence Scenario

The Pre-Independence Period

The post-Independence scenario of tea in Barak Valley when it compared with the Brahmaputra Valley reveals a very unimpressive picture. Today the general feeling among the tea planters of Barak Valley is that Brahmaputra Valley enjoys some geo-structural advantages which help it record better performance than Barak Valley in tea production. The climate and soil conditions are often cited as the reason for the better performance by tea gardens of some Brahmaputra Valley districts like Lakhimpur, Dibrugarh, Darrang etc. But the historical evidences of tea cultivation in Assam in its initial stage (i.e., mid 19th century) do not substantiate such arguments. Tea cultivation in the erstwhile Cachar district was started a decade later than the then Assam. It soon flourished and Cachar was in no way behind rest of Assam. During the nineteenth century, Cachar tea was holding the top position in production among the districts of Assam. In 1869 Cachar had 24151 acres under tea and yielded 4255000 lbs. For some years up to 1876 however, the production of Brahmaputra Valley advanced more rapidly than that of the Surma Valley (Sylhet & Cachar) but since then the balance dramatically reversed. (Bhattacharjee 1997). In 1882 the area under cultivation in Cachar had risen to 48873 acres and the productivity to 12721000 lbs which was the highest production from any district of Assam. The annual growth rates during this period were as high as 15.5% and 23% for area under tea and production respectively. In 1885, of the total production of 53617020 lbs of Assam province, Surma Valley with only two districts of Cachar and Sylhet, yielded

20998978 lbs while Brahmaputra Valley which had seven districts could produce only 32618042 lbs. Of the tea producing districts in Assam, Cachar topped the list and was followed by Sibsagar, Lakhimpur and Sylhet. In respect of tea gardens also Cachar had the distinction of having highest number of tea gardens with 199 nos. followed by Sibsagar 174, Lakhimpur 141 and Sylhet 133. In 1900 the area under tea cultivation in Cachar was 61179 acres with an average productivity of about 500 lbs of made tea.

Table 2.1

District-wise Growth of the Tea Industry in Assam

(figures in thousand acres)

District	*Acreage under tea*						
	1883	*1900*	*1920*	*1935*	*1945*	*1950*	*1955*
Sylhet	28	71	91	89	6	-	-
Cachar	50	61	63	53	75	75	73
Goalpara	-	1	1	4	4	4	4
Kamrup	6	4	4	4	5	5	5
Darrang	17	42	57	61	62	64	64
Nowgong	11	13	13	12	12	13	13
Sibsagar	41	78	99	103	104	109	106
Lakhimpur	37	68	61	109	112	116	118
Total	109	337	420	435	373	386	386

Source: Digest of Tea Statistics, 1971-72.

In the sphere of export and price the performance of Cachar tea was very bright. India was the largest exporter of tea and Cachar was holding a dominant position. In 1865 at an exhibition in Paris, where Indian indigenous goods including tea was displayed, the sample of Cachar tea was highly admired and the manager of Lalamukh Tea Estate was rewarded for quality manufacture (Bhattacharjee 1977). In the price front Cachar tea were fetching very good price and strong enough to resist any price and demand crash. We can quote the remarks of John Smeal, part proprietor of several tea gardens in Cachar, to the then Commissioner in 1968, "...our teas have fetched a very high price, averaging last year in London, rupees 125 a mound. Rupees 60 per mound is a common average price in London for Cachar Tea" (Griffith 1967). Despite affect of crisis in 60s, the whole tea industry of Cachar exhibited a comparatively better performance in partially resisting the crisis and making possible an early revival. The opinion of Edger (Griffith 1967,) made in 1873 is of worth mention here: "To that keen observer, the prospect of tea seemed more hopeful in Cachar than any other district. Edgar's main ground for this belief was that the planters of Cachar 'seemed to have made more progress than any other district utilizing scientific method in cultivation and manufacture for the crude experiments which caused more loss in earlier times. He also appears to have considered the climate of Cachar more suitable to tea than that of Assam Valley or the Terai (Griffith 1967).

Being lured by the success of tea production in Cachar in the 19th century speculative activities started to take place in Cachar. The operational success and the official reports engendered the most extravagant belief in tea as a money spinner. It had been thought that any one could run a tea garden. People were recklessly purchasing any land at exorbitant prices without considering economic viability of tea production. Soon they discovered how foolishly they had started gardens were and dismayed by the realization of profit. Besides ill considered speculation, other factors responsible for less profit or loss were, lack of restraint on the part of the government in granting land resulting in gardens in unsuitable areas, lack of experience and competence on the part of the entrepreneurs regarding cultivation and manufacture, insistence of many proprietors on quantity which affected quality. Panic started to spread swiftly and there was a wild rush to sell resulting in frequent change in ownership which was detrimental to growth of tea industry. This situation became worse in the post-Independence period, when many sound companies started to withdraw their capital from here. A picture of change in ownership of the sick gardens in Cachar District (erstwhile) since 1940 has been presented in Table 2.2.

Table 2.2
Change of Ownership Since 1940

Name of the tea estate	No. of time
1. Pathechera	1
2. Haticherra	2
3. Sree bahula	1
4. Subang	3
5. Bhuban Valley	1
6. Benodnagar	2
7. Chincoorie	4
8. Saraswati	Nil
9. Monierkhal	1
10. Ballacherra	1
11. Saibona	3
12. Rahamannagar	Nill
13. Lakhipur	1
14. Chorgola	4
15. Singlacherra	2
16. Isabheel	1
17. Longai	2
18. Coombhira	3
19. Bidyanagar	3
20. Pathini	2
21. Sonaicherra	2
22. Durganagar	Nill
23. Madancherra	Nill
24. Raomanikrishna	3
25. Maniknagar	3
26. Rajarampur	Nill
27. Madanpur	Nill
28. Rabhania	1

Source: Tea Directory of various years

As motive of owners of tea gardens in Cachar was to earn maximum profit with minimum effort, the gardens were not nourished properly. There was very little effort made for regenerating the production capacity of the bushes as well as the soil both of which have some limits of their capacity beyond which the health of the gardens starts to deteriorate. The tea bushes have some 'economic age' after which its productivity starts to fall both quantitatively and qualitatively. Unless some amount of profit is ploughed back in activities like plant replacement, infilling, rejuvenation etc. an economic garden turns uneconomic. The 'economic age' of tea bushes varies marginally in between variety of plants and location of garden. "In mid-Assam it is suggested that 34 to 40 years is the maximum useful life of a section of indigenous Assam tea plant. Under similar conditions a Manipuri or Burma kind more common in Cachar might last for 40-45 years'. In most gardens in Cachar, tea plants of even 30 years represent between 60 percent and 70 percent of the whole garden and in some cases even more as in 1949. (Cachar Plantation Committee Report 1950 p. 8). Whereas in Assam, replacement of old and worn out tea plants has been a regular feature, in Cachar less attention seems to have been paid to this important matter.

It is very important to apply fertilizers most judiciously for a series of years to maintain the fertility of soil even in the economic gardens. Manuring is a continuous process. After long gap, if suddenly overdose manure is applied, this may adversely affect the soil. Suppose, on a poor area, in the past receiving say, 30 lbs nitrogen, a sudden increase to 80 lbs would largely be wasted. The aim should be to build up the bushes gradually by increased doses of fertilizer application. "At present (1948) part of the reasons for the season's low yields in certain gardens in Cachar is due to the fact that they have been in the past plucked hard for crop and starved of nitrogenous manures" (Cachar Plantation Committee Report 1950, p. 15). Manure which is very important especially for the types of soil attainable in Cachar, was long neglected and inorganic manure was possibly not used till 1911, i.e., nearly 64 years after the gardens were started. (Cachar Plantation Committee Report 1950, p. 62)

According to Manna "as a general policy it is by no means wise to have manifest deterioration before going to manuring. A slightly continuous decrease in productivity is a warning that the land is less capable of producing than it was. According to ITA, Sub-Committee report published in 1948, "it is apparent that natural manure alone will not step up crops sufficiently on the poorer gardens of Cachar to cover the present day high working cost and produce a profit". The Committee further stated that "the Managers appear to be universally agreed that the lack of manure, more especially inorganic fertilizers is one of the prime causes of low, out-turn... Many agencies, however, have been reluctant to apply such fertilizers as have become available due to the higher cost and the low nitrogen content of the mixture on offer." The value of manure was not only insufficiently realized but there are instances of application of unsuitable substances like lime which was most harmful to the tea plant. Although Tocklai Institute was opened in Cachar in 1911, it was not till 1925 that the discovery of this harmful effect of lime was known. Commenting on this Harler said, "in the decade or so, over which it (like) had been employed much money and crop had been lost, and in some cases, persistent heavy liming had seriously crippled gardens" (Cachar Plantation Committee Report 1950, p. 63).

The productivity per acre of Cachar and Lakhimpur (the highest yielding district of Assam), was almost same up to 1900, and a gap was created and started to widen steadily since the date from which the practice manuring first began. In the second quarter of twentieth century gap started to grow most rapidly, the period in which Assam was marked by better cultural methods and intensified manuring while Cachar was much slow to take advantage of this. Comparative average yields in 1948 were:

Region	*Productivity*
Lakhimpur	12½ mds per acre
Assam (including Cachar)	10-11 mds per acre
Cachar	7 mds per acre

The district-wise growth of the industry in Assam from the year 1883 to 1955 was as follows.

Table 2.3
Acreage under Tea

(figures in thousand acres)

Districts	*1883*	*1900*	*1920*	*1935*	*1945*	*1950*	*1955*
Sylhet	28	71	91	89	6	-	-
Cachar	50	61	63	53	75	75	73
Goalpara	-	1	1	4	4	4	4
Kamrup	6	4	4	4	5	5	5
Darrang	17	42	57	61	62	64	64
Nowgong	11	13	13	12	13	13	13
Sibsagar	41	78	99	13	104	109	106
Lakhimpur	37	68	61	109	112	116	118
Total	189	337	420	435	373	386	386

Source: Digest of Tea Statistics, 1971-72, pp. 4-5

NB: Cachar includes Cachar (present), Hailakandi and Karimganj districts Lakhimpur includes Dibrugarh and Lakhimpur (North) districts.

It is observed in the above table that the progress of Cachar tea during this period is very unimpressive while the other districts like Lakhimpur, Sibsagar marked quite significant progress. Cachar even had some decline in acreage during the period from 1920 to 1935 by 10 thousand acres and from 1950 to 1955 by 2 thousand acres. The acreage growth rate of Cachar during the period was 46% (0.52) whereas that attained by Lakhimpur district was 218%. The overall growth rate of acreage attained by Assam was 104%.

In Cachar during the period from 1929 to 1949 there were about 110 tea estates out of which 56 gardens were owned by Indians. Out of the total acreage under tea of about 75000, the Indian-own estate represented barely 22 percent. Out of 56 gardens under Indian ownership not more than half a dozen estates with a total registered acreage of about 1200 were Indian enterprises in origin. The rest were purchased by the Indians from the Europeans when they found it unremunerative to hold any longer. There were instances where the purchasers paying only 10 percent of the purchase money got the balance from banks paying interests at rates varying from 6% to 9% per annum. Purchase of gardens at inflated and even, should we say, "fancy" price with bank money were greatly responsible for financial difficulties of quite a large number of Indian owners in taking proper care of the gardens. Banks not only charged higher rate of interest but they also did not advance adequate fund and hypothecation to run the garden properly not to speak of making improvement thereon. As a result, years after years the property deteriorated. What was more, in their anxiety to repay the bank loans or realise return of capital invested, the Indian owners extracted the maximum in minimum of time even at the cost of the health and life of the plant or up-keep of the soil. While the Indians generally suffered from lack of adequate finance, their European counterparts had a little scope to make grievance of want of fund. There was a noticeable reluctance on their part in further investment for reasons best known to them (Cachar Plantation Committee Report 1950, p. 71). In some quarter this is attributed to transfer of affections while other opines political compulsion and a feeling of uncertainty. All these together caused fall of production years after years and gradually it turned out to be a losing proposition to run the gardens. Taking advantage of the Tea Control Act (1933) and the ready market for "anything" produced, investors generally did not lose and they some how suck-out enough to get back the money invested with good margin of profit. But to this valley it turned out to be a great loss. The valley which was a leader in tea production in all respects during the beginning of tea production in Assam was lagging much behind the other districts of Assam. It got the stigma of the region of 'uneconomic tea gardens'. This state of affairs left this region at the end of first half of the 20th century with as many as 16 nos. of uneconomic tea gardens. They were:

---

1. Arcuttipore
2. Binnakandy
3. Binodini
4. Silcoorie and Poloi
5. Kuttal
6. Singalta

7.	Lallamukh
8.	Chorgola, Singhacherra and Maguracherra
9.	Kallaincherra
10.	Tuillak
11.	Binnakandy
12.	Borakai
13.	Bora Jalinga
14.	Rosekandy
15.	Goombira
16.	Eraligool

Source : Cachar Plantation Committee Report 1950, p. 3.

The table 2.4 depicts price fetched and productivity per acre by some uneconomic and profit earning gardens during the period 1938 to 1948.

The Table 2.4 shows that there was not much variation in respect of quality reflected by price fetched between non-economic and profit-making gardens. What made the difference was the average productivity. Average productivity of only one un-economic garden was above 8 lbs whereas in case of profit-earning tea gardens average productivity of only one was less than 8 mds. Another significant feature observed is that, all the profit-earning gardens attained some steady growth in their productivity, only one uneconomic garden i.e., Borakhai could achieve some considerable increase in productivity and six of them had to face fall in their productivity during the period from 1938 to 1948.

Location of Uneconomic Gardens

It is most interesting to note the actual location of the uneconomic gardens and to see whether the uneconomic gardens fall on the uneconomic zones deteriorated on the basis of the following criteria.

a) Weak tea on southern and south western slopes of *teelas.*

b) Tea on *teelas* whose top soil has been eroded away due to faulty methods of cultivation in the past.

c) Tea on sunken *bheels* subject to regular flood

d) Tea on badly drained clay flats, specially where these flats have been regularly silted up.

Table 2.4
Price of Tea and Yield per Hectare (1938-1948)

Name of the garden/ownership	*Price per lb./Anna*								*Average productivity / acre)*			
Uneconomic Tea Estates	*1938*		*1946*		*1947*		*1948*		*1938*	*1946*	*1947*	*1948*
	As.	*P.*	*As.*	*P.*	*As.*	*P.*	*As.*	*P.*	*Mds.*	*Mds.*	*Mds.*	*Mds.*
Silcoorie & Poloi (Jardine Henderson)	9	7	15	7	19	0	21	8	6.4	4.7	4.3	5
Kuttal (KcLeod & Co)	8	2	15	4	19	3	21	4	8.0	5.6	7.2	7.9
Singalla (Jardine Henderson)			15	11	19	5	21	8		6.0	5.7	6.7
Lallamook (Jardine Henderson)			15	3	19	2	21	10		5.1	5.1	5.5
Chargola, Singalacherra & Maguracherra (James Finlay)			15	3	18	9	21	1		5.3	5.2	5.4
Kallincherra (Octavious Steel Co.)	8	2	14	8	18	3	19	1	4.6	4.8	5.3	5.4
Tilkah (Octavious Steel Co.)	8	3	15	4	20	2	21	9	5.0	5.7	5.2	5.0
Binakandy (Octavious Steel Co.)	8	0	15	3	20	4	22	10	5.8	5.8	5.5	5.4
Borokai (Duncan Bros.)	9	1	15	8	18	6	19	11	4.3	5.8	6.8	8.9
Boro Jalinga (James Finlay)	7	9	14	10	19	10	20	10	7.7	6.4	6.5	5.7
Rosekandy (Duncan Bros.)	8	10	15	3	17	6	21	4	4.4	4.7	4.2	4.3
Arcuttipore (Gillanders Arbuthnot)	7	7	17	6	19	0	21	2	4.3	4.7	4.6	4.0
Goombira (James Finlay)	9	2	15	7	19	4	21	8	8.0	6.3	6.1	6.9

Profit-earning Tea estates												
Endogram (Octavious Steel Co.)	9	8	15	6	19	1	21	7	5.0	8.0	8.4	8.6
Sonai River (Davenport & Co.)	7	5	14	7	18	11	20	7	10.3	7.8	8.5	10.2
Kalline (Duncan MacNeil & Co.)	7	10	15	3	18	9	20	10	7.8	10.7	10.3	11.0
Rukni (Walter Duncan & Co)	9	5	17	0	19	8	22	9	6.4	9.5	9.4	10.4
Burnie Braes & Serispore (Jardine Henderson)	8	0	16	7	19	6	22	0	6.3	7.0	7.0	6.6
Chandighat (Duncan Bros.)	7	11	16	5	18	9	21	8	7.6	9.5	8.6	9.0
Roopcherra (McLeod & Co.)	7	11	15	6	19	5	21	5	5.3	5.9	8.2	9.9

Source: Cachar Plantation Committee Report 1950, pp. 89-90

e) Very poor areas containing poor mixed hybrid tea.

f) Old tea due for uprooting within the next few years.

Out of the sixteen uneconomic gardens that existed in Cachar in 1948, six were in Chatla *Bheel* and six in Hailakandi and Chargola circles. Two were in Lakhipur in the south of the Barak river. One was in Happy Valley north of the Barak, but was almost the southern most garden in the circle. In the north Cachar (north of the Barak) there was only one garden which had failed to show a profit in 1948 (Cachar Plantation Committee 1950, p. 11). Thus almost all the non-economic estates were located in the south of Barak river and on the better soils in North and North West Cachar. With only two exceptions made profit in 1948. North of the Barak river, in addition, the drought effect was much less serious than in the more southern areas. The point that needs to be stressed here is that the climatic and soil conditions could not be blamed as the major reason for making the gardens uneconomic in Barak Valley.

Leaving the climate and soil, other major cause may be inadequate ploughing back of profits, which happened to be the main cause of industrial sickness in many cases. The observation of the Cachar Plantation Committee (1950, p. 28) would be of much relevance:

"In some cases, despite loss the reserves of the (uneconomic gardens) companies were distributed in dividends. These, however, are probably estates which will soon either go out of production entirely or at least be worked in future only on a small scale by non-resident labour."

Regarding the low quality of Cachar tea reflected by low price fetched, the committee also observed that

"a) fine plucking will invariably produce teas of better quality than coarse plucking;

(b) the amount and condition of withering, the number of rolling tables and of firing machinery and their condition and efficiency has a very considerable effect on the quality of the teas produced. It may, however, be stated that within limits, those gardens whose factories are run efficiently and in which particular attention is paid to cleanliness obtained appreciably higher prices per pound for their teas than those whose factories are less efficiently run and less cleanly maintained."

3

Tea Cultivation in Barak Valley, Brahmaputra Valley & India: A Comparative Analysis

The above facts and observations take us to the conclusion that proper care of the garden by the management accompanied by required amount of timely investment can keep the garden healthy thus accruing large amount of profits. But unfortunately the scenario did not mark any change during post-Independence period also. In some respect the situation has rather been aggravated. The number of uneconomic tea gardens in Cachar has increased taking the figure of sick tea estates in this valley to 28 nos. Though the acreage and production of tea in Barak Valley have shown some increase, the pace is much slow when compared with Brahmaputra Valley and India. The Table 3.1 gives a picture of the growth of area and production of tea in Barak Valley as compared with Brahmaputra Valley and India during the period 1951 to 1995.

The time series data as presented in the above table indicates an increase between 1951 to 1995 in respect of area and production of tea in Barak Valley, Brahmaputra Valley and in India. The trend of 'area expansion' and production in linear and exponential form are presented in Table 3.2 to Table 3.7 for the regions Barak Valley, Brahmaputra Valley and India. The graphical presentation of trends of area expansion and production are in Annexure 1 and 2 respectively.

Table 3.1: Area and Production of Tea (1951-1995)

Year	*Area ('000 hectares)*			*Production ('000 kg.)*		
	Barak Valley	*Brahma-putra Valley*	*India*	*Barak Valley*	*Brahma-putra Valley*	*India*
1951	30.4	125.2	316.8	19.8	130.4	285
1961	29.9	132.4	331.2	20.2	162.1	354
1971	31	151.3	356.5	22.7	201	435
1972	31.3	152.9	359	24.8	214.4	456
1973	31.3	153.8	360	25.7	226.1	471
1974	31.4	156	362	28.3	237	489
1975	31.5	157	363	27.6	235.4	487
1976	30.9	158.4	364	31.5	244.8	511
1977	31.1	159.5	366	33.1	260.1	556
1978	31.4	161	369	29.2	267.8	571
1979	31.9	163.6	373.7	28.3	255.6	543
1980	32.2	168.4	381.8	31.5	269.2	569
1981	32.4	170.6	383.6	29.3	275.9	560
1982	33.4	177.9	394.2	30.7	268.4	560.7
1983	33.5	179.5	96	32.5	289.2	581.4
1984	33.9	180.8	98.5	33.8	304.7	639.9
1985	33.8	181.3	399	33.4	319.2	656.2
1986	34.7	187.9	407.6	34.2	301.2	620.8
1987	34.9	190.9	411.3	30.6	333.1	665.3
1988	35	192.5	414.3	33.6	335.8	700
1989	35	194.4	415	39.1	340.7	688.1
1990	35	190.2	416.2	40.2	342	720.3
1991	35.3	192.4	420.4	40.6	353.1	754.2
1992	35.3	192.5	420.3	41.2	363.4	732.3
1993	34.4	191.7	418.3	42	361.4	760.8
1994	35.7	194	423.5	42.3	350.1	743.8
1995	35.2	193.5	422.2	42.9	349.2	754
2001	32.7	269.1	509.8	49.7	402.7	853.9
2007	32.3	321.3	578.4	44.1	467.7	986.4

Source: Indian Tea Association, Surma Valley Branch,Silchar

In order to analyse the present status of 'tea production' in this Valley we have made a comparison of 'area under tea' and 'total production' between three regions Barak Valley, Brahmaputra Valley and India. Data relating to the above objectives were collected for the period 1951 to 1995. In analyzing the trends, the base year has been considered as 1951. Several growth patterns as well as methods of their computation are available in the past literature. But one should not consider any growth pattern arbitrarily without examining its suitability to any relevant situation. In fact, the growth rates may be of different types as mentioned below :

a) constant amount of increase or decrease

b) varying amounts but at constant ratio of increase and decrease.

Growth curves, viz., linear and exponential are available for analyzing the time series data under the above two different situations. The linear regression is suitable for a time series data involving constant amount of change. Exponential curve is useful for analyzing a time series data having constant ratio of change. The functional form of linear and exponential are as follows.

(1) Under linear $T_t = a + b_t$

(2) Under exponential $T_t = ab^t$

In selecting a particular form the above two models in analyzing, the following consideration was made.

To ensure whether the mean of the differences of a series is zero or not, we have used the statistical test as mentioned below:

a) For linear form, ΔT_t = constant = C_1 (say)

Which is equivalent to Average of $\Delta C = 0$

So, for examining whether linear form can be selected as a good fit or not, the null hypothesis

H_0 (average of $\Delta C_1 = 0$) may be tested. Considering $\Delta C_1 = X_1$

The test statistics is $t = \dfrac{\overline{X}_1 - 0}{S_1/\sqrt{n_1}}$ with $(n_1\text{-}1)$d.f. where $\overline{x}_1$ is the average of X_1 and S_1 in the standard deviation of X_1 n_1 is the number of observation.

b) For exponential, $\Delta \log T_t$ = constant = C_2 (say)

So, for examining whether exponential form can be selected as good fit or not we test the null hypothesis H_O (Average of $\Delta C_2 = 0$).

Considering $\Delta C_2 = X_2$

The test statistics is $t = \frac{\overline{X}_2 - 0}{S_2 / \sqrt{n_2}}$ with $(n_2\text{-}1)$d.f.

where $\overline{x}_2$ is the average of X_2 and S_2 is the standard deviation of X_2. N_2 is the number of observations.

Now, to select a growth curve which will be the best fit to any situation, there is no statistical test is choosing a specific form as a best fit in comparison to others, because of the fact that the theory of testing of hypothesis tells us to accept or reject any null hypothesis, against the specific alternative. So, to accept the particular form as a best fit, the principle of dispersion has been considered. Here we have considered the principle of measuring the dispersion of a statistics "D" where 'D' is the difference in absolute term between the observed value and estimated trend value based on any trend equation.

i.e., "D" = Observed value – estimated trend value

From the values of standard deviation of the variable D, we can select a particular curve as the best fit if the value of standard deviation for that form is the lowest amongst all models considered.

In order to decide the type of trend which will fit the time series data adequately and which may be a logical description of the said time series data, we have attempted first with the help of test statistics 't' as explained earlier. Simultaneously, we have also estimated the trend values based on the above two types of trend model and have arrived at the standard deviation of statistics 'D'.

Table 3.2: Trend of Area Under Tea in Barak Valley

Model	*Value of 't'*	*d.f*	*Specification of equation*	*Table 't' at 5%*	*SD of 'D's*
Linear	0.00280	26	y_t=29.877+0.2239t	1.721	0.822631
Exponential			y_t=(29.969)(0.0068)^t		6.106255

Linear model accepted

Table 3.3: Trend of Area Under Tea in Brahmaputra Valley

Model	*Value of 't'*	*d.f*	*Specification of equation*	*Table 't' at 5%*	*SD of 'D's*
Linear	5	26	y_t=138.13+2.3846t	1.721	3.4729
Exponential			y_t=(140.01)(1.0144)^t		30.07121

SD of 'D' suggests linear model but 't' test does not support.

Table 3.4: Trend of Area Under Tea in India

Model	*Value of 't'*	*d.f*	*Specification of equation*	*Table 't' at 5%*	*SD of 'D's*
Linear	0.48309	26	y_t=336.23+3.6118t	1.711	5.350239
Exponential			y_t=(337.7)(1.0095)^t		6.255623

Linear model accepted.

Table 3.5. Trend of Production of Tea in Barak Valley

Model	*Value of 't'*	*d.f.*	*Specification of equation*	*Table 't' at 5%*	*SD of 'D's*
Linear	0.1496	26	y_t=20.976+0.7938t	1.721	1.332
Exponential			Y_t=(21.989)(1.0257)^t		30.07121

Linear model accepted.

Table 3.6: Trend of Production of Tea in Brahmaputra Valley

Model	*Value of 't'*	*d.f.*	*Specification of equation*	*Table 't' at 5%*	*SD of 'D's*
Linear	0.457321	26	y_t=175.03+7.5713t	1.721	1.332
Exponential			y_t=(181.49)(1.0296)^t		41.59738

Linear model accepted.

Table 3.7: Trend of Production of Tea in India

Model	*Value of 't'*	*d.f.*	*Specification of equation*	*Table 't' at 5%*	*SD of 'D's*
Linear	2.4761	26	y_t=371.25+15.452t	1.711	1.332
Exponential			y_t=(386.01)(1.0286)^t		20.57816

Linear model accepted.

A perusal of the above tables reveal that in the case of Barak Valley linear model is the 'line of best fit' among the two for presenting the growth of both area and production as it satisfies both the criteria of SD of 'D' and 't' test at 5% level. In Brahmaputra Valley test 'D' suggests the selection of linear model for area and through 't' test does not support the same. In case of India linear model suits both the criteria for representing both area and production.

The 'b' in the linear model y = a+bt, represents the growth rate. So, it appears from the above that the tea industry around which the economy of Barak Valley revolves, has not made any convincing progress during the post-Independence period both in respect of expansion and production in comparison to other two regions. When the area under tea in Assam and India made much progress, Barak Valley remained almost stagnant. Rate of increase of total production in Barak Valley is much below the relevant rate in Assam and India. The lower rate of increase in production of Barak Valley tea is mainly due to very small increase in area and partly due to low rate of increase in productivity rate.

The above table shows that in 1951 the average productivity of tea in Cachar was lowest at 651 kg/ha among the tea producing districts of Assam (Table 3.8). While in that period other districts of Assam like Darrang, Goalpara and Lakhimpur attained a rate of more than thousand, at which Cachar has reached long after 40 years. But during this period by better cultivation and field practices those districts of rest of Assam, have raised their average productivity to a level of around 2000 kg/ha. The districts of Lakhimpur and Dibrugarh which were competitors of Cachar in the nineteenth century are in average productivity rates of 1849 and 2195 kg/ha respectively as in 1995, whereas Cachar was found staggering at a rate of 1341 kg/ha at that point of time.

Table 3.8: Average Productivity of Tea in Assam and Other Places in India

(in kg/hectare)

District/state	*1951*	*1961*	*1971*	*1981*	*1991*	*1992*	*1993*	*1994*	*1995*
Darrang	1063	1177	1336	1655	2016	2053	2049	2004	1999
Goalpara	1102	1071	1158	1386	1697	1855	1032	1976	1820
Lakhimpur	1193	1460	1605	1901	1962	1927	1900	1844	1849
Dibrugarh				2048	2135	2223	2171	2093	2195
Cachar	651	647	733	904	1150	1167	1224	1296	1341
Total Assam	966	1123	1227	1503	1717	1763	1770	1764	1779
Terai	759	990	1203	1395	1697	1484	1738	1909	1896
Dooars	1711	1222	1359	1581	1732	1737	1865	1816	1755

Source : Tea Statistics 1956-57.

Size-wise Area and Production of Tea Estates

The size group of 200-400 hectares covers 45.5% of the total tea area in Barak Valley and contributes 36.9% of the total tea production. Size group up to 100 ha contains 28 nos. of gardens covering 942 hectares of area contributing 3.3% of the total area. This group of gardens produces a total of 469 thousand kgs which is 1.4% of the total production as on 31.12.95. The size group of 100 to 200 hacters, covers 6.1% of the total area and contributes 4.4% of the total production. The gardens belonging to the size group of above 400 hectares holds 45.3% of the total tea area in Barak Valley, producing 57.5% of the total production. It follows from the above analysis that gardens of largest size group dominate the tea production in Barak Valley. The same situation prevails in the Brahmaputra Valley.

It follows from the above table that productivity of tea in Barak Valley is much lower in comparison to that of Brahmaputra Valley irrespective of the size group of garden. Smaller tea gardens in Barak

Table 3.9: Size-wise and Production of Tea in Barak Valley, Brahmaputra Valley and Assam in 1995

Regions/ State	*Size of Gardens*																			
	Upto 100 ha				*100 to 200 ha*				*200 to 400 ha*				*Above 400 ha*				*Total*			
	No. of estates	*Area*	*Prod- uction*	*Producti- vity/ ha*	*No. of esta- tes*	*Area*	*Prod- uction*	*Producti- vity/ ha*	*No. of esta- tes*	*Area*	*prod- uction*	*Producti- vity/ ha*	*No. of esta- tes*	*Area*	*Prod- uction*	*Producti- vity/ ha*	*No. of esta- tes*	*Area*	*Prod- uction*	*Producti- vity/ ha*
Brak Valley	28 (24.34%)	942 (3.14%)	469 (1.16%)	497	14 (12.17%)	1819 (6%)	1767 (4.4%)	971	48 (41.73%)	13628 (45.5%)	14845 (36.9%)	1089	25 (21.73%)	13580 (45.3%)	23099 (57.48%)	1700	115 (100%)	29969 (100%)	401180 (100%)	1340
Brahma- putra Valley	587 (54.30%)	11053 (5.32%)	16871 (4.65%)	1526	127 (11.74%)	18237 (9.28%)	30077 (8.29%)	1649	155 (14.33%)	46040 (23.45%)	85288 (23.53%)	1852	212 (19.6%)	120981 (61.62%)	230201 (63.51%)	1902	1081 (100%)	196311 (100%)	362437 (100%)	1846
All Assam	615 (51.42%)	11995 (5.3%)	17340 (4.30%)	1445	141 (11.78%)	20056 (8.86%)	318844 (7.90%)	1587	203 (16.97%)	59668 (26.36%)	100133 (24.86%)	1678	237 (19.81%)	134561 (59.46%)	253300 (62.89%)	1882	1196 (100%)	226280 (100%)	402617 (100%)	1779
Producti- vity in Barak valley as % of all Assam's avg. Productivity			34.43%				61%				65.9%				90%				75.32%	

Source: Tea Statistics 1995-96

Valey are found to be more inefficient and less productive when compared with all Assam. The tea estates in the largest size group in Barak Valley are more efficient, whose efficiency index, is above 90% of the Assam average. One of the important feature is that most of the large gardens in Barak Valley are under public sector or FERA ownership. This implies that public sector gardens and gardens under FERA ownership are more productive in comparison to other categories.

Age Group of Bushes

Age of tea bushes is an important index of health of tea estates. It is also an indicator of low rate of investment in the garden for the purpose of plantation. Large number of uneconomic tea bushes is detrimental to the development of tea estates. The low rate of average productivity in Barak Valley is considered to be the effect of higher number of tea bushes over the 'economic age'. In Barak Valley about 47.58% of the tea bushes were above the 'economic age' of 50 years

Table 3.10: Age Group of Bushes During 1978 in Barak Valley

Age group	*Area covered (hec)*	*Percentage to total*
Below 5 years	1940	6.41
6 – 10	2192	7.24
11 – 20	3675	12.14
21 – 30	2291	7.56
31 – 40	2645	8.74
41 – 50	3123	10.33
Above 50	14403	47.58
All age groups	30269	100.00

Source: Techno-Economic Survey of Cachar 1982

as in 1978 (Table 3.10). It may however, be mentioned in this connection that Assam and north India contained 68.42% and 61.35% of the total area under bushes in the economic age-group of less than 50 years in 1993 (Table 3.11). The area covered by over-aged bushes of these two regions stood at 31.58% and 38.65% respectively.

In order to get a relative picture of the aspect age of tea bushes, the figures of Brahmaputra Valley and India are also, shown in the Table 3.11 for four years 1978, 1983, 1988 and 1993.

Table 3.11: Age Group of Bushes During 1978-1993 in Barak Valley

Age of tea bushes in years	*Barak Valley*				*Brahma-putra Valley*	*Assam total*	*All India*
	1978	*1983*	*1988*	*1993*	*1993*	*1993*	*1993*
0-5	6.4	7.2	7.5	8.7	7.2	7.5	7.7
5-10	7.2	8.4	9.0	11.3	10.6	10.7	9.9
11-20	12.1	11.5	10.8	14.6	14.8	14.8	13.4
Subtotal (0-20)	25.7	27.1	27.3	34.6	32.6	33.0	31.0
21-30	7.6	9.2	11.9	11.1	14.7	14.2	13.4
31-40	8.7	7.0	8.4	9.3	13.1	12.5	11.9
41-50	10.3	10.8	9.5	6.8	8.9	8.6	8.0
Subtotal (21-50)	26.6	27.0	29.8	27.2	36.7	35.3	33.3
Over 50	47.6	45.9	42.8	38.1	30.6	31.7	35.7
Grand total	100	100	100	100	100	100	100

Source : Statistical profile of Barak Valley 1999

It is observed from Table 3.11 and 3.12 that very little progress has been made in reducing the percentage of 'uneconomic bushes' during this period as the figure was 47.6% in 1978 which has been reduced to 38.1% in 1993 but still this figure is much higher when compared with 30.6% of Brahmaputra Valley and 35.7% of all India. The significant rise in number between the age group 5-10 indicate that during last 10 years some substantial plantation has taken place in this valley though much is yet to be done.

Cost of Production and Price Realisation

Cost of production and price realization are the major parameters to evaluate the economic viability of any tea estate. The cost of production of tea in Barak Valley is comparatively lower than Assam and some other tea producing regions for the last five years from 1990 to 1994 as shown in Table 3.12. The table gives a bird's eye view of the cost of production in some tea growing regions in India for five years from 1990 to 1994.

Table 3.12: Cost of Tea Production in Different Regions 1990-1994

(*Rs/ kg*)

Region	*1990*	*1991*	*1992*	*1993*	*1994*
Barak Valley	27.30	29.91	34.05	47.02	40.97
Assam	35.12	40.17	47.34	51.42	51.07
Darjeeling	91.77	105.35	123.00	127.38	154.41
Dooars	35.80	38.20	43.74	46.11	46.08
Terai	30.88	34.56	41.04	44.11	41.06
South India	35.05	38.19	46.28	43.40	41.83

Source: Tea Statistics 1996

Unfortunately, Barak valley could not reap benefits of this low cost as the price fetched by 'Cachar Tea' produced in Barak Valley are also abnormally low (Table 3.13). In some years the price fails to cover even the cost leading marginal gardens to the verge of closure. The tea of Barak Valley suffers from the stigma of 'Cachar Tea' meant poor quality tea. Due to this stigma even the better-quality tea from Barak Valley finds it difficult to fetch a better price which it actually deserves.

Table 3.13: Average Price (Rs./kg) at Gauhati Auction Market

Year	*Barak Valley*	*Brahmaputra Valley*
1990	39.44	45.53
1991	34.58	44.34
1992	34.54	41.70
1993	45.97	51.46
1994	33.20	45.79

It is observed from the tables that 'Cachar Tea' always fetches much lower price than that of Assam Valley. Comparing the cost of production of Cachar tea as shown in Table 3.12 with their corresponding prices fetched as shown in Table 3.13, it is found that the profit margin of Cachar tea is very small. This small margin of profit is a serious problem affecting the overall growth of tea cultivation in this valley.

In the year 1993 and 1994, more strangely the tea gardens in Barak Valley had to face a situation when average price per kg was less than the cost incurred. Such state of affairs is undoubtedly a matter of great concern for any industry. The public limited companies and other financially strong gardens may manage to survive for some years in this situation but such casualties become irreversible in the case of marginal gardens. Barak Valley has been no exception in this regard and as a result in 1995 Barak Valley ended up with as many as 28 nos. of sick tea estates.

4

Impact of Industrial Sickness on the Economy

Introduction

Industrial sickness has grave socioeconomic consequences. It leads to loss of employment, production and blockage of scarce resources of the country. The increasing trend of sickness adversely affects the investment climate in the country and causes loss of revenue to the exchequer. It also adversely affects the profitability of banks and financial institutions through loss of interest on these advances. This causes depletion of earning potential due to blockade of funds and increases administrative expenses. A massive industrial sickness thus, eats into the vitals of the economy making it a high-cost-low-productivity economy which is, incapable of competing in the world market. Though sickness is a common feature all over the world, it is more a serious problem in developing countries than in developed countries. A developed country with its wide net of social security measures can easily safeguard the interest of the affected workers, but not necessarily in a country like India due to poor social security measures. Since unemployment is a major problem in India, workers once thrown out of employment join the stream of the millions of employment seekers and find it difficult to get employed. On the other hand, a country where resources are scarce and at minimum, cannot afford to waste them also.

Adverse Impact of Industrial Sickness on the Indian Economy: A Review in the Interregional Comparative Perspective (With Special Reference to Financial Aspects and Employment Position)

Sickness of an industry causes loss of valuable scarce national resources like land area, machinery and equipment, bank resources, etc. It is very difficult to give a correct estimate of the loss of resources like land area, machinery etc., as accounts of these are not maintained systematically. To present an idea on loss of resources, the aspect of bank resources is discussed below:

At a time when India was in great crisis due to shortfall of financial resources to its requirements, various austerity measures were taken and the people were asked to sacrifice rigorously to solve the crisis and save country's sovereignty, a huge amount of investable resources in the form of bank credit were locked up in sick industrial units. As per information compiled by RBI from commercial banks, as on 31st March 1998, bank credit blocked in sick units was to the tune of Rs. 15682 crores as against Rs. 13,787 crores in 1997. (Economic Survey of India 1999-2000, pp. 51-52). The small scale sector blocked Rs. 3857 crores (24.7 per cent) in its units while the non-SSI sector Rs. 11825 crores (75.4 per cent). Bank credit blocked in the non-SSI sector in private, public and joint/cooperative units were Rs. 8109 crores, Rs. 3014 crores and Rs. 702 crores respectively.

Our country is of diverse character. Different regions do not exhibit same feature. Hence, this discussion will be incomplete if the offence of this crime is not examined from regional perspective. This aspect has been exhibited in the Table 4.1.

Table 4.1 shows figures of number of sick small scale and non-SSI units and amount outstanding to commercial banks of India in four regions: Eastern (including North Eastern), Northern, Western (including Central Region) and Southern Region for the year 1998. The Eastern region is very unfortunate to bear the burden of major part (48.17%) of the total no. of sick small-scale industrial units of the country; but it has blocked least portion (16.82%) of the total outstanding credit for which Western region is the main offender blocking 31% of the amount outstanding. However, this situation is entirely different in case of non-SSI sick industrial units. Non-SSI sick units in percentage is least in Eastern Region as against worsted regions such as Western and Southern Region. Eastern Region is blocking the least portion of the outstanding credit in non-SSI units as in small scale units. Resources blocked up in sick units in India is a major cause of increasing non-performing assets of the commercial banks of India. A non-performing

Table 4.1: Position of Sick Small-Scale and Non-SSI Industrial Units in 1998*

(Rs. in crores)

State/Union Territory	*Small scale units*		*Non-SSI units*	
	No. of sick units	*Amount outstanding*	*No. of sick units*	*Amount outstanding*
1. Eastern Region	106756 (48.17)	648.96 (16.82)	419 (16.92)	1879.58 (15.89)
Andaman & Nicobar Is.	45	1.60	0	0.00
Arunachal Pradesh	456	0.94	2	2.47
Assam	15774	60.62	44	157.97
Bihar	24935	142.74	63	358.24
Manipur	1919	8.79	2	2.42
Meghalaya	4076	6.52	2	1.39
Mizoram	615	2.45	0	0.00
Nagaland	1386	4.98	2	4.48
Orissa	1889	35.63	57	210.64
Sikkim	33	0.11	1	6.35
Tripura	2011	6.26	6	9.41
West Bengal	53617	378.32	240	1126.21
2. North-eastern Region	40579 (18.31)	954.97 (24.76)	526 (21.24)	2472 (20.90)
3. Western Region	33758 (15.23)	1137.57 (24.49)	767 (30.97)	3563 (30.13)
4. Southern Region	40443 (18.25)	1115.14 (30)	764 (30.85)	3910 (33)
All India (1+2+3+4)	221536 (100)	3856.64 (100)	2476 (100)	11825.25 (100)

* Figures in the parentheses denote percentage to total.

Source : Report on currency and finance, 1998-99.

asset in India represents an advance that has not been serviced as a result of 'past dues' accumulated over 180 days and more which is a major cause of erosion of banks' profitability in India. Up to the period of 1997-98, the percentage of NPA of public, private and foreign banks were 8.2%, 5.3% and 2.2% of the total advance (Economic Survey of India 1999-2000, pp. 51-52). A district-wise break up of the credit outstanding of the banks in Barak Valley and Assam is given in the Table 4.2. The amount of outstanding credit in Barak Valley stands at Rs. 15160 lakh which is about 6% of the total outstanding credits in Assam.

Table 4.2: Outstanding Credit of Commercial Banks in Barak Valley

District/State	*No. of offices*	*Outstanding credit*
Cachar	72	8821
Hailakandi	20	1575
Karimganj	47	4764
Barak Valley	139	15160
Assam	1269	205320

Notes: Figures in the parentheses denote percentage to all Assam.

Source : Currency and Finance 1998-1999, pp. 41-42.

The industrial sickness is causing serious damage to the economy of the country in terms of resource and employment loss. As on March 1996, it was very widespread, afflicting 2.64 lakh units in almost all industries across the states and the union territories (GoI 1996-1997). This excludes 1.26 lakh non-existent and non-traceable SSI units with an outstanding bank credit of Rs. 240 crores. These 2.64 lakh sick units employed about 55-60 lakh persons (Mehta, 1992). The losses of 117 out of 240 central government undertakings were estimated to be Rs. 5287 crores in 1993-94, employing 7-8 lakh persons. The aggregate scene of industrial sickness including public and private sectors in India amounts to a magnitude of around 2.75 lakh units (a very large number of them terminally sick) with total loss of about Rs. 31000 crores and employing about 7-8 million people (Mehta *et al.* 1999).

Effect of Industrial Sickness on the Economy of Barak Valley

The effect of industrial sickness specially of tea estates, on the economy of Barak Valley is very serious. The Barak Valley which has hardly any worth mentioning industry is largely dependent on its tea industry for income, employment and revenue generation. In 1996, the daily average number of labourers employed in tea gardens of Barak Valley was 71716 and about 250000 persons were dependent on tea industry for earning their livelihood. Though tea industry in this valley has a great potential for employment generation, with 16074 hectares (47% of the total grant area) still available for expansion, the industry is performing far from expectation (Indian Tea Association, Silchar).

The incidence of unemployment has been very high in the tea estates of Barak Valley. Exact number of current unemployment in tea gardens of Barak Valley is very difficult to present due to non-availability of data. So, we present here a comparative picture of unemployment in Barak Valley, Brahmaputra Valley and Total Assam as on 1958, (Table 4.3).

The Table 4.3 shows that when percentage of unemployment to the total labour force was 9.0% in Brahmaputra Valley that figure was as high as 14.6% in the case of Barak Valley and 9.6% at the level of Assam. Table 4.4 shows that labour employment per hectare was higher in Barak Valley, i.e., 3.86 compared to 3.61 of Brahmaputra Valley in the year 1900. This fell to 1.67 in Barak Valley as against 2.53 of Brahmaputra Valley in 1992. Though during the next period upto 1997 the situation improved pushing up the figure to 2.24 in 1997, still the relevant rate was lower in comparison to Brahmaputra, all Assam and all India situations. The situation is bound to retard due to large scale crash in the coming years in the face of liberalisation policy of the government. Some sick gardens in Barak Valley which could come out of sickness before liberalisation have now been forced back to their earlier position adding to the miseries of the labourers including production and resource loss.

Table 4.3: The Incidence of Unemployment in the Tea Gardens of Assam

(person per thousand in labour families)

	Brahmaputra Valley			Barak Valley			Total of Assam		
	M	*F*	*Total*	*M*	*F*	*Total*	*M*	*F*	*Total*
1. Employed* person	303.19	252.98	556.17	39.70	28.40	68.10	342.89	381.38	624.27
2. Unemployed person	26.59	28.18	54.77	6.70	4.80	11.60	33.29	33.08	66.37
3. Persons in labour force* (1+2)	329.78	281.16	610.94	46.40	33.30	79.70	376.18	314.46	690.64
4. Persons outside labour force	252.63	237.29	489.92	44.60	39.50	84.10	297.23	276.79	574.02
5. Total labour population (3+4)	582.41	518.45	1100.86	91.00	72.80	163.80	673.41	591.25	1264.66
6. Percentage of unemployment to the labour force	8.1	10.0	9.0	14.4	14.7	14.6	8.9	10.5	9.6
7. Percentage of unemployment to the total labour population	4.6	5.4	5.0	7.4	6.7	7.1	4.9	5.8	5.3
8. Percentage of persons in labour force to the labour population	56.6	54.2	55.5	51.0	45.7	48.7	55.9	53.2	54.6

Source: Report on the Sample Survey of Unemployment Situation in the Tea Gardens of Assam, 1958.

Table 4.4: Employment per hectare in Tea Estates

Year	*Labour employed/ hec under tea*			
	Barak Valley	*Brahmaputra Valley*	*Assam total*	*All India*
1900	3.86	3.61	3.69	3.40
1901	3.13	3.70	3.57	3.29
1906	2.71	3.26	3.03	2.66
1926	2.64	3.43	3.13	2.86
1950	2.52*	3.50*	3.31*	3.26*
1961	1.77	2.92	2.70	2.48
1966	1.74	2.60	2.45	2.33
1971	1.50	2.32	2.18	2.15
1972	1.53	2.28	2.15	2.12
1973	1.51	2.23	2.11	2.13
1974	1.55	2.26	2.14	2.13
1975	1.52	2.25	2.13	2.13
1976	1.56	2.24	2.13	2.13
1977	1.58	2.27	2.15	2.15
1978	1.57	2.31	2.19	2.18
1979	1.72	2.39	2.28	2.25
1980	1.52	2.38	2.24	2.22
1981	1.55	2.39	2.26	2.21
1982	1.52	2.32	2.19	2.19
1983	1.52	2.30	2.18	2.18
1984	1.57	2.33	2.21	2.21
1985	1.54	2.38	2.25	2.24
1986	1.58	2.29	2.18	2.19
1987	1.58	2.28	2.17	2.20
1988	1.90	2.40	2.32	2.37
1989	1.87	2.46	2.37	2.36

1990	1.70	2.47	2.35	2.37
1991	1.72	2.49	2.38	2.37
1992	1.67	2.53	2.40	2.36
1993	1.70	2.51	2.39	2.37
1994	1.84	2.57	2.46	2.41
1995	2.09	2.57	2.51	2.41
1996	2.43	2.52	2.51	2.39
1997	2.24	2.56	2.52	2.38

* Calculated on the basis of area under tea in 1951.

Source: Mazumdar (ed.), 2001, 'Tea Industry in Cachar : A Statistical Profile', in *Centenary Souvenir* (1901-2001), Surma Valley Branch Indian, Tea Association.

Impact of Sickness on Tea Plantation Units: Some Case Studies

While attempting to show the extent of damage done to the economy due to sickness in tea gardens in Barak Valley a presentation of the state of affairs in some particular sick gardens is made below. The situations in other sick gardens' are almost alike.

Pathini Tea Estate

Pathini is one of the tea estates of Karimganj district situated at the international border with Bangladesh. The management of this garden was transferred to Tea Trading Corporation of India from its earlier management - M/s Octivious Steel and Company Ltd. in 1975. This garden which was earning profits earlier, since then has been moving towards sickness. The situation has become so bad that the sickness of this garden is alleged to have caused the death of 17 of its labourers due to starvation (*Dainik Jugasankha*, 28 June, 2001). Non-payment and irregular payment of wages and rations in the garden were regular phenomenon. The following facts and figures clearly show the extent of loss due to sickness in this garden, which is the common effect of sickness in any garden.

Table 4.5: Effect of Industrial Sickness in Pathini Tea Estate

Extent of loss	*As on 31.12.75*	*As on 31.12.93*
Area	2374 hectare	2374 hectare
Area under tea	810 hectare	550 hectare
Total employees (all category)	2000 nos.	1800 nos
Tea made	7 lakh kgs.	4 lakhs kgs.
Medical officer/Asstt. Medical officer	4	1

Due to lack of proper treatment, replantation and feeding of existing bushes by fertilisers/chemicals etc. the condition of tea bushes deteriorated affecting the quality of tea produced. Due to poor maintenance the existing factory became unfit for production of tea. During the year 1993 plucking had to be suspended for 15/16 days for want of machinery and shortage of coal,. HSD etc. which affected quality and quantity of produce. Machinery like dryer, rotorvane, chimney established long ago met with no proper renovation and became less efficient. There were four generator sets in the factory. One Blackstone engine now is in disrepair. Out of three Kirloskar engines, one has totally collapsed. The rest two engines need thorough overhauling with rennovation. A good number of trucks, jeeps, ambassador cars, motor cycles are not in running condition. Two tractors are running somehow in a very poor condition.

Wages and rations on which the labourers live are very irregular. In 1993 continuously for 3 weeks and 2 months wages and salaries were not paid and ration was also not issued properly. There was backlog of ration to workers for about 2/4 weeks.

PF contribution and LIC premium deducted from salary are not deposited to the concerned authority in time. PF authorities filed case against the management, the retired employees are deprived of getting their PF dues in time. Gratuity has also not been paid to the eligible employees for the last 5/6 years (Memorandum by employees/workers/ representatives, Pathini TE 23 Feb, 94). During the period from 1975 to 1993 while non-sick gardens made some expansion in area under tea, marginal increase in labour employment and quite substantial increase in production, this garden exhibited reverse trend (Table 4.5). The area under tea declined by 260 hectares. Most serious was the loss of jobs of 200 labourers which has made their families completely incomeless. Loss of production was of the tune of 3 lakh kgs. All these produced a far reaching effect on the regional economy.

Chincoorie Tea Estate

This garden, located at a distance of about 10 km from Silchar town, is in the grip of sickness for a couple of decades. Total area of this estate is 1327 ha out of which 160 ha are under tea cultivation. Presently this garden produces green leaves in only 47 hectares. At present this garden is under the control of Deputy Commissioner, Cachar, the management being entrusted to a cooperative society. This garden has been continuously incurring loss. Cumulative losses of the garden till 1995 reached about Rs. 90 lakhs. Full wages have not been paid to the workers for the last 2 years. Other outstanding dues (including payments due to 'Statfed' and PF liabilities) amount to around Rs. 2 lakhs.

Chincoorie had a factory which has since long (1975) become defunct. Owing to paucity of funds, maintenance of the garden has suffered badly with the consequence that the production of green leaves is falling down drastically. The last pruning and cultivation works were carried out in 1993. Around 113 ha of cultivable land has been converted into jungle leaving the present cultivation confined to only 47 hectares. The annual financial requirement for the mere survival of this garden has been estimated to be Rs. 23 lakhs, whereas the income from it could not meet even 1/3rd of it. This garden would have been closed 15 years back, had it not received Rs. 52 lakhs from ONGC from the sale of 51 hectares of land to it. This amount was largely spent for clearing outstanding dues leaving a meagre amount for its revival. In such a stage large number of jobless labourers are maintaining themselves in a painfully bad condition by cultivating vegetables working as wage earners at other places other than tea gardens.

Conclusion

The scenario in the other sick gardens are as gloomy as that of the two gardens discussed above characterised by huge loss of investable resources, loss of production and large scale unemployment. The figures of employment maintained in the office records of the sick gardens do not reflect the actual position because the immediate casualties of sickness are the casuals labourers who constitute the major portion of the total employment in a garden. The next victims are permanent labourers. Though their names are not deleted from the employment registry of gardens, they to face untold miseries. Their salaries become very uncertain and supply of ration, cloth etc. and also bonus become irregular or discontinued. This economic disease does not remain confined to the gardens, it seriously jeopardises the whole economy of the region. It would be right to say that one of the major causes of underdevelopment in Barak Valley is the widespread industrial sickness in its tea gardens.

5

Sickness in Tea Industry of Barak Valley: Causal Factors

In the preceding chapters the analysis of the causes of 'industrial sickness' in tea industry of Barak Valley are based on the individual cases of tea estates. Now we have to make an general analysis of the causal chain. Some of the causes, such a acute competition, market recession etc. which are common to the industry as a whole in the market economy have not been repeated here though their relevance are not overruled at all. But the main focus of this chapter is to bring out Barak Valley specific causes. Secondly, almost all the causes are interlinked – cost overrun leads to diversion of funds, leading to inadequate working capital, low capacity utilisation, poor sales, reduced dues payment capability (including PF), labour unrest etc. Over and above of all these, there has been decline in production; and working capital has become more scarce. Lastly, there are cases of tea estates where the major cause of sickness has been natural calamities like flood, earthquake etc. Sometimes and in some cases the causes are socio-political in nature including law and order problem and the problem of terrorism. These are the common factors affecting all the gardens in the valley and hence, on this consideration they are not brought to discussion in the present study. The main objective of this chapter is to know why some gardens are performing quite successfully while others are not, in spite of the fact that they are working under same conditions like same climatic condition, soil composition, geographic location etc. Even there are instances of two adjacent gardens where one is quite sound and another is weak/sick. Some of these sick gardens had been performing well in two decades back, for instance, Pathini Tea Estate. Our study will target the following specific factors and examine their role in the sickness of tea estates in Barak Valley.

Management

The role of entrepreneur or management has been the very core of the history of industry and industrial development in the world. How business enterprise is managed is vital and the success or failure of a firm depends on it to a large extent. In fact, the major credit for tremendous industrial development in the 20th century should be given to the 'Management Revolution' that took place (Banerjee 1970). It has been realised that in the absence of proper kind of management, business enterprise cannot be run efficiently. Impact of good management on efficiency, productivity, cost of production and human relations has widely been accepted. In the western advanced economies scientific management has already become the way of life in the field of business and industry.

According to G.R. Terry (Dave 1987) 'management is a distinct process consisting of planning, organising, actuating and controlling, performed to determine and accomplish the objectives by the use of people and resources'. E.F.L. Brech (Brech 1965) states, 'management is concerned with seeing that the job gets done and done efficiently'. J.L. Lundy (Lundy 1968) views "Management is principally a task of planning, coordinating, motivating, and controlling the efforts of others toward a specific objective. It involves the combination of the traditional factors of production (land, labour and capital) in an optimum manner, paying due attention of course, to the particular goals of the organisation." In the words of Harold Koontz and Cyril O'Donnel, (Dave 1987) "Perhaps there is no more important area of human activity than managing, for it is the task of the manager to establish and maintain an internal environment in which people working together in groups can perform effectively and efficiently toward the attainment of group goals".

Thus, 'management' embraces many functions such as planning, organising, staffing, directing, co-ordinating, controlling, motivating etc. Each and every function has got its own importance and at the same time all of them taken together need to be performed in a scientific way for getting desired results in the most economical and efficient manner.

Earlier it was believed that 'managers are born'. Planning a business enterprise was considered a function which could be done by intuition, by the sons and relatives of businessmen and industrialists. The father of modern management is the French industrialist Henri Fayol (Dave 1987). His keen observations on the principles of general management first came in 1916, in French language under the title 'Administration Industrielle et Genarale'. This magnificent book was not translated into English until 1929. Thus Fayrol reflecting his ideas based on his long managerial experience observed that management is a technical process which can be taught. Thus, management is neither an exclusive privilege, nor a particular responsibility of the head of senior members of the business. Management is a skill, which is to be acquired and operated along with other apparatus. In the context of the present world we may say, a more qualified manager if provided with sufficient managerial infrastructure like supply of data, information technology and skilled co-human skills will productivity better result, otherwise, hardly, better result from any industrial unit can be expected. So, in order to diagnose the causes of sickness of an industry one most important step would be to analyse first the management aspect of that industry.

At the present economic environment of open and competitive economy, the application of scientific management is very vital for the survival and growth of various industrial units. The difference between 'scientific management' and 'traditional management' lies in the manner in which decisions are made. One need not be a technologist in order to perform 'scientific management'. What is needed is that all the decisions should be based on facts and figures developed by a scientific approach towards all the problems to be faced in business. This is quite contrasted to predicting decisions solely on opinions, prejudices and unsound rule of thumb. According J.L. Lundy, the scientific method of management can be summarised briefly as follows:

1) Recognise the problem, analyse it, and define objectives,
2) Gather and analyse the necessary data,
3) Synthesise possible alternatives,
4) Review and evaluate each alternative,
5) Test conclusions, if possible,

6) Take selected actions,
7) Review results and, if necessary, correct action,
8) Formulate and test principles based on experimental results of many cases.

In this chapter, the effort to study the effect of poor management on the performance of gardens faced with the difficulty of cardinal measurement of 'managerial efficiency'. One way to evaluate the 'management' could be the assessment of the intellect, perception and profession quality of the manager by interacting with them and consideration of their qualifications. The degree of error in such type of subjective evaluation may be more which demands more caution. Along with them the presence of other features of 'scientific management' are taken into consideration.

In practising the above procedure in evaluating 'managerial efficiency' in the gardens a complicated situation is faced in Assam and more particularly in Barak Valley.

Measuring the extent of 'scientific management' practised in the tea gardens specially in Barak Valley is not a very easy task. Different factors that need to be considered, are educational qualification and service experience of the managerial persons, their ability and intelligence. Above all, it requires the scrutiny of the method of management, in order to know whether the procedures and steps involved in 'scientific management', are followed or not. Among the above mentioned factors ability, intelligence etc. pose some quantification problems.

As regards the qualification and experience, the personal interview and official records do not provide clear picture. This is due to the fact that, in the tea industry, even today, there is no definitely laid down method by which qualified candidates are recruited to executive posts. A manager is generally selected more on extraneous considerations than on merit. This was the practice even at the early stage of the tea industry in Assam. C.A. Bruce, the brother of Robert Bruce, who is usually credited with the discovery of tea plants in Assam as early as in 1823 (IRC 1835) is said to have possessed little knowledge of botany and horticulture or any special qualification for the post, although he was appointed as the Superintendent of the experimental gardens in July

1836, on a salary of Rs. 400 per month (IRC 1836). Edward Money (Griffith 1967, p. 97), writing in 1870 "…new gardens were commenced on impossible sites and by men as managers who were not only ignorant about tea plants but also about the commonest rules of agriculture.' Tea planters in those days were a strange medley of retired or cashiered army and navy officers, medical men, engineers, veterinary surgeons, streamer captains, chemists, shop keepers of all kinds, stable keepers, used up police men, clerks and goodness knows what besides". The present scenario is also not much different which could impress us of improvement of managerial efficiency. Considerations, other than the field efficiency still dominate the recruitment of managerial persons. Referring to the standard of candidates recruited by estates. D.H. Lacock, the then Director of Tocklai Experimental Station said, (Two Leaves and a Bud 1970, Feb, p. 64) "The modern agricultural world is becoming more and more technically competent but increasingly complex. You should not shut your eyes to these inevitable developments and I strongly suggest that the time has come for estates to recruit youngsters with agricultural or other suitable degrees." Lacock expressing dissatisfaction over the appointment of poor quality of managers the Director goes on to say, "There is really no excuse at all because science graduates are by no means in short of supply. This is 1970, not 1895 and a nephew with a degree in music is not what we need, delightful and charming as the fellow may be. I must state quite fearlessly that our selection of candidates will not be affected by sentimental consideration' (Two Leaves and a Bud, Dec 1970).

An estate following the principle of 'scientific management', besides, if equipped with good quality of managerial staff is certain to do its best in utilising the available resources. Though during 'depression the synchronising may not be completely evaded, the magnitude of damage would be less and would attain its normal position in a relatively lesser period of time. Here it has been attempted to examine the extent of 'scientific management' practiced along with the quality of manpower (managerial) in different gardens, of Barak Valley. On the basis of this criteria, the gardens have been categorised into four groups viz., very-efficient-management, efficient-management, average-management and below-average-management. Efforts have been made to minimise the error as much as possible but the existence of subjective elements like human sincerity, devotion, farsightedness etc. throw hurdles to reach to complete error-free conclusions. Such classification of management needs to be tested to find whether they are properly classified or not. For examining this the gardens with different management categories along with respective average productivity for four representative years were put in tabular form as below:

Table 5.1: Management-wise Average Yield of Tea

Type of Management	*1985*	*1990*	*1995*	*1998*
Very-efficient-management	1820	1923	2171	2526
Efficient-management	1206	1460	1166	1519
Average-management	718	1086	1043	1610
Below-average-management	984	937	960	1524

Source : Tea Board of India, Silchar

In order to test the significance of the above classification we have taken the null hypothesis.

H_0 = Managements do not differ significantly.

Now, by applying F-test for Two-Way Classification, it is found that the calculated value of F is 41.78 (Annexure 3). This calculated value is greater than the tabulated value at 5% level of significance with 3, 15 degrees of freedom, hence, the null hypothesis is rejected and concluded that the different categories of management are significantly different from each other (Table 5.1).

The estates after being classified into 4 different efficiency levels of management are again placed into nine different size classes (tables 5.2 to 5.5)

The above tables indicate the distribution of tea estates according to size and category of management in four different years 1985, 1990, 1995 and 1998 respectively. The average productivity of class as well as maximum and minimum productivity of the estates belonging to each classes are also shown in these tables.

Table 5.2: Distribution of Tea Estates according to Size and Category of Management during 1985

Category of management/ type of ownership	*Management category I*				*Management category II*				*Management category III*				*Management category IV*			
Size/class (hec)	*No. of estate*	*Min yield*	*Max yield*	*Avg. yield*	*No. of estate*	*Min yield*	*Max yield*	*Avg. yield*	*No. of estate*	*Min yield*	*Max yield*	*Avg. yield*	*No. of estate*	*Min yield*	*Max yield*	*Avg. yield*
Upto 100									3	100	399	280	9	80	1721	603
100 – 200	1	1891	1891	1891	3	323	2185	1000	21	199	199	199	6	98	1497	764
200 – 300	1	1665	1665	1665	15	492	2405	947	45	327	1536	1117	6	485	805	650
300 – 400	2	1700	1971	1835	5	311	1700	1315	1	1043	1048	1048	3	497	1971	1338
400 – 500					7	913	2159	1553	2	538	1283	910	5	895	1648	969
500 – 600					3	926	957	945								
600 – 700	1	1889	1889	1889	2	1042	2000	1524	1	755	755	755	1	1579	1579	1579
700 – 800					2	1038	2116	1577								
800 – 900					1	1161	1161	1161								
900 – 1000					1	833	833	833								
Total	5	1786	1853	1820	39	782	1502	1206	13	495	870	718	30	606	1240	984

* Management categories I, II, III & IV refers to Very-efficient-management, Efficient-management, Average-management & Below-average-management respectively.

Source : Indian Tea Association, Silchar, Individual survey by the researcher.

Table 5.3: Distribution of Tea Estates according to Size and Category of Management during 1990

Category of management/ type of ownership	*Management category I*				*Management category II*				*Management category III*				*Management category IV*			
Size/class (hec)	*No. of estate*	*Min yield*	*Max yield*	*Avg. yield*	*No. of estate*	*Min yield*	*Max yield*	*Avg. yield*	*No. of estate*	*Min yield*	*Max yield*	*Avg. yield*	*No. of estate*	*Min yield*	*Max yield*	*Avg. yield*
Upto 100					1	1417	1417	1417	2	211	471	341	4	288	577	465
100 – 200					3	419	1904	1000	4	171	2466	1328	5	102	746	214
200 – 300					10	549	1792	1238	7	616	1895	1418	5	400	1512	1000
300 – 400	2	1928	2055	1991	5	570	1936	1397	6	102	1893	777	3	650	1533	983
400 – 500	1	1897	1897	1897	7	921	2946	1757	3	338	2002	1283	1	616	616	616
500 – 600	1	1186	1186	1186	4	828	1313	1139					1	1186	1186	1186
600 – 700	1	1614	1614	1614	3	887	2305	1386	2	49	1796	1372				
700 – 800	1	2210	2210	2210	1	2660	2660	2660								
800 – 900					2	1021	1288	1154					1	847	847	847
900 – 1000																
Total	6	1186	2210	1923	36	419	2946	1460	24	102	2466	1086	19	102	1533	937

* Management categories I, II, III & IV refers to Very-efficient-management, Efficient-management, Average-management & Below-average-management respectively

Source: Indian Tea Association, Silchar, Individual survey by the researcher

Table 5.4: Distribution of Tea Estates according to Size and Category of Management during 1995

Category of management/ type of ownership	*Management category I*				*Management category II*				*Management category III*				*Management category IV*			
Size/class (hec)	*No. of estate*	*Min yield*	*Max yield*	*Avg. yield*	*No. of estate*	*Min yield*	*Max yield*	*Avg. yield*	*No. of estate*	*Min yield*	*Max yield*	*Avg. yield*	*No. of estate*	*Min yield*	*Max yield*	*Avg. yield*
Upto 100					1	835	835	835	2	255	469	362	4	155	2126	677
100 – 200					2	609	726	668	2	351	1383	867	1	719	719	719
200 – 300					10	614	2335	987	7	542	1833	1116	2	948	1524	1236
300 – 400	2	2026	2225	2125	5	786	1808	1302	2	926	1335	1130	3	579	1315	978
400 – 500	2	1893	2031	1962	8	1013	2757	1786	1	1314	1314	1314	2	630	700	665
500 – 600					3	996	1072	1045					1	1486	1486	1486
600 – 700									3	1220	1615	1470				
700 – 800*	1	2427	2427	2427	3	782	2498	1453								
800 – 900					1	1254	1254	1254								
900 – 1000																
Total	5	2115	2227	2171	33	861	1519	1166	17	768	1325	1043	13	753	1311	960

* Management categories I, II, III & IV refers to Very-efficient-management, Efficient-management, Average-management & Below-average-management respectively

Source: Indian Tea Association, Silchar, Individual survey by the researcher.

Table 5.5: Distribution of Tea Estates according to Size and Category of Management during 1998

ategory of* management/ type of ownership	Management category I				Management category II				Management category III				Management category IV			
Size/class (hec)	*No. of estate*	*Min yield*	*Max yield*	*Avg. yield*	*No. of estate*	*Min yield*	*Max yield*	*Avg. yield*	*No. of estate*	*Min yield*	*Max yield*	*Avg. yield*	*No. of estate*	*Min yield*	*Max yield*	*Avg. yield*
Upto 100					3	652	2223	1292	3	517	914	787	7	204	1614	767
100 – 200	1	3615	3615	3615	1	584	584	584	1	1825	1825	1825	4	291	1825	1234
200 – 300					14	914	2741	1455	5	965	2374	1537	4	908	1336	1130
300 – 400	1	2423	2423	2423	6	677	2685	1391	4	703	3642	2252	3	867	3151	1828
400 – 500	2	1808	2169	1989	7	1207	3162	1799	3	1444	1852	1688	2	866	900	853
500 – 600	1	2009	2009	2009	4	997	2112	1355	2	536	1551	1044	1	2009	2009	2009
600 – 700					1	2664	2664	2664	1	2345	2345	2345	1	2345	2345	2345
700 – 800	1	2596	2596	2596	3	389	2610	1679	2	1034	2000	1517	1	2000	2000	2000
800 – 900					1	1453	1453	1453	1	1502	1502	1502				
900 – 1000																
Total	6	2490	2563	2526	40			1519	22			1610	23			1524

*Management categories I, II, III & IV refers to Very-efficient-management, Efficient-management, Average-management & Below-average-management respectively

Source : Indian Tea Association, Silchar, Individual survey by the researcher

It is revealed from Tables 5.2 to 5.5 that tea estates with very-efficient-management belong to the size group of 200 to 800 hectares whereas 80% of estates in efficient-management category belong to 200 to 700 size group. In the average-managed category about 80% of the gardens are of below 400 hectares size. Estates of below-average-managed level are mainly of small size as 92% of them are of below 500 hectares. Even some are of below 100 hectares also. Whereas very well managed gardens begin from the size above 300 hectares.

The gap between minimum and maximum productivity (in kg/hec) has been found to be very high constantly from 1985 to 1990 in the case of all categories of management except the very efficient category of management. This situation became acute in 1990, when minimum and maximum productivity in respect of the efficient-managed, average-managed and below-average-managed gardens were 419 and 2946, 102 and 2466 and 102 and, 1533 respectively. This situation has not much changed in 1998, except for some increase in minimum productivity however keeping the magnitude of gap almost unaltered.

The Tables 5.2 to 5.5 reveal another aspect. That though the better management reflected better average yield, but that again was not consistent in all the years. Only the average productivity for very-efficient-managed estate was much higher in all the four years. The difference was not much significant for other three categories specially in the years 1985 and 1998. The inconsistency in results referred to above may partly be ascribed to random factors. Such random influences are always found in time series data. But there may be other significant causal factor playing their role. In order to identify these important factors we have conducted some statistical tests.

For testing the existence of relationship between productivity and sizes, we have used the test statistics 't',

where, $t = \beta.Exy/(MSE^*)^{1/2}$ ... ... 5(a)

with degrees of freedom (d.f.) equal to d.f. of SSE*.

Here, y = average productivity and x = size of estates.

This is in fact a test of $H_0(\beta.=0)$.

The result of test statistics 't' are presented in Table 5.6.

Table 5.6: Statistical Results

Year	*Value of 't'*	*d.f.*
1985	21.4467	26
1990	389.79738	26
1995	475.09578	26
2000	744.24878	26

* Significant at 1% level.

The positive value of 'β.' (table 5.7 – 5.10) as well as significant value of test statistics 't' (Table 5.6) suggest that there is a significant positive relationship between productivity and size.

In order to take care of the effect of holding size being associated with type of ownership, we have taken the help of the technique of Analysis of Convenience. By this technique, we have examined whether variation in productivity between the four different types of ownership is due to differences in ownership type or due to its dependence on the size of the estates which also varies from one type of ownership to the other. The relevant null hypothesis is:

H_0 = Average productivity does not differ between types of management.

The results of the ownership efficiency analysis are presented in the Tables 5.7 to 5.10. The values of test statistics 'F' suggest to reject at 5% level the null hypothesis of equality of average productivity under different types of management even after considering the dependence of productivity on size.

Table 5.7: Analysis of Co-variance of Table 5.2

Sources of variation	*df*	SS_{xx}	SP_{xy}	SS_{yy}	*Estimated "β"*	*Adjusted*	*df*	*For testing absence of any relationship*
Size	9	98.57	-6818.67	1997607.3	10.95			
Ownership	3	50.65	-3673.92	13531745				
Error	27	110.78	1210.59	-10245240		-10258469	26	
Total error	39	260	-9282	5284112		3248921	38	
Ownership + error	30	161.45	-2463.33	3286505		13507391	12	2.85

Note: Significant at 5% level.

Table 5.8: Analysis of Co-variance of Table 5.3

Sources of variation	*df*	SS_{xx}	SP_{xy}	SS_{yy}	*Estimated "b"*	*Adjusted*	*df*	*For testing absence of any relationship*
Size	9	82.24	10968	17251747	15.40			
Ownership	3	24.84	493	8684657				
Error	27	37	570	-4093650		-4102431	26	
Total error	39	144.08	12031	21842754		4591007	38	
Ownership + error	30	61.84	1063	4591007		8675165	12	4.58

Note: Significant at 5% level.

Table 5.9: Analysis of Co-variance of Table 5.4

Sources of variation	*df*	SS_{xx}	SP_{xy}	SS_{yy}	*Estimated "b"*	*Adjusted*	*df*	*For testing absence of any relationship*
Size	9	48	690	3146093	37.95			
Ownership	3	19	-2821	3329247				
Error	27	60	2277	-348403		-434815.15	26	
Total error	39	127	146	6126937		2977098	38	
Ownership + error	30	79	-544	2980844		3411913	12	17

Note: Significant at 5% level.

Table 5.10: Analysis of Co-variance of Table 5.5

Sources of variation	*df*	SS_{xx}	SP_{xy}	SS_{yy}	*Estimated "b"*	*Adjusted*	*df*	*For testing absence of any relationship*
Size	9	125	-12299	4484965	64.45			
Ownership	3	37	-9148	4457425				
Error	27	64	4125	3711124		3445255	26	
Total error	39	226	-17322	12653514		7918742	38	
Ownership + error	30	101	-5023	8168549		4473487	12	2.81

Note : Significant at 5% level

For testing the equality of average productivity between two types of management at a time we have applied 't' statistics as follows:

$$t = \frac{y_i - y_j}{\sqrt{MSE * \left(\frac{1}{n_i} + \frac{1}{n_j}\right)}} \text{ with d.f. n-4} \quad \ldots \quad \ldots \ 5(b)$$

where,

y = average productivity,

i & j = types of management,

n = number of estates

The results of the above test statistics 't' are shown in Tables 5.11 to 5.14.

Table 5.11: Values of Test Statistics 't' Defined as in 5(b) for Testing Equality of Yield between the Management (year 1985)

	Very efficient management	*Efficient management*	*Average management*
Very efficient management			
Efficient management	1.65		
Average management	2.77*	1.50	
Below average management	2.10*	0.68	-0.75

* Significant at 5% level.

Table 5.12: Values of Test Statistics 't' Defined as in 5(b) for Testing Equality of Yield between the Management (year 1990)

	Very efficient management	*Efficient management*	*Average management*
Very efficient management			
Efficient management	2.13*		
Average management	3.56*	1.82*	
Below average management	4.36	2.66*	0.68

* Significant at 5% level.

Table 5.13: Values of Test Statistics 't' Defined as in 5(b) for Testing Equality of Yield between the Management (Year 1995)

	Very efficient management	*Efficient management*	*Average management*
Very efficient management			
Efficient management	3.12*		
Average management	3.36*	0.48	
Below average management	3.61*	1.20	0.30

* Significant at 5% level.

Table 5.14: Values of Test Statistics 't' Defined as in 5(b) for Testing Equality of Yield between the Management (Year 1998)

	Very efficient management	*Efficient management*	*Average management*
Very efficient management			
Efficient management	5.06*		
Average management	5.45*	-0.54	
Below average management	4.91*	-0.028	0.49

* Significant at 5% level.

The Tables 45.11 – 5.14 reveal that the average productivity of the estates with 'very efficient management' is significantly different from other three categories of less efficiently managed gardens in all the four years. Though in 1985 the difference of average productivity between 1st and 2nd category management gardens is not very significant at 5% level. The average productivity between 2nd, 3rd and 4th category of estates are not much different. Only in 1990, the difference of average productivity between 'Efficiently-managed' estates with 'Average-managed' and 'Below-average-managed' estates shows some significance. It has also been observed that number of gardens under the 1st category remained unchanged at 5 or 6, but other gardens are frequently changing their ranks among three other types of management as observed from change of total number of estates under 2nd, 3rd and 4th category over the years. It proves that improving the management to the level of 1st category is not quite easy and once attained that will certainly result into a very high level of average productivity quite at par with the well performing gardens of upper Assam and in other parts of India.

Another significant matter that has been observed in Table 5.2 to 5.5 is that though we have included all the 28 sick gardens in our study, the number of estates under the 'below-average' category of management are not always 28 or more, while the figure is 30 in 1985, it is found to be 19, 13 and 23 in the years 1990, 1995 and 1998 respectively. It indicates that all the sick gardens are not managed at below-average level, some are better managed but could not increase their yield. This fact along with the existence of wide gap between minimum and maximum productivity within the same category of management indicates the operation of some other concomitant factors causing low productivity in tea estates. Some of these factors may be uneconomic age of tea bushes, ownership change, insufficient finance, absence of tea processing units, court cases etc. The existence of these factors in various sick gardens is discussed later.

Investment and Finance

A firm whether large or small, owned by an individual proprietor or share holder is dependent largely on capital for the smooth functioning of it. Inadequate finance happens to be a major cause of industrial sickness in maximum cases, so the remedy of sickness also lies on the provision of adequate finance. Tea is one of the very few commodities whose production involves both agricultural and manufacturing processes. Like many agricultural items, the original fertility of land is not the principal factor dominating the production of tea, both in qualitative and quantitative terms. Here the producer should ensure some other services like re-plantation, rejuvenation and consolidation work, provision of adequate irrigation and drainage, application of fertilisers, controls of weeds, plant diseases and pest, pruning, maintenance of standard plucking round etc. If the above mentioned activities are stopped for some period (may be due to paucity of finance), the health of the garden will sure to be affected and this may lead to sickness. Once sick, multiple efforts are required to revive the garden from the year long accumulated deficiencies on the above heads, where the need for money is multiplied. The problems of the sick gardens of Barak Valley are often of above-mentioned nature. In these gardens these mentioned activities were not carried out for a long time for financial and/or other constraints. The age of 50% of the bushes in Barak Valley are above the economic age (i.e. 50 years) and the re-plantation rate is very low at 0.5 percent as against suggested rate of 2% per annum. These are significant indicators of under investment on tea cultivation in this valley.

The present chapter seeks to examine the impact of investment on productivity in the tea estates as because productivity (both quantitative and qualitative) is the main factor which may aggravate sickness or effect revival of any garden. From the cost structure depicted in the balance sheets of various gardens the researcher reached the conclusion that investment on cultivation head might have most powerful and direct impact on the yield. The cultivation (old and new) includes new plantation, re-plantation, rejuvenation, pruning, irrigation and drainage, protection against weeds and plant diseases and pest control, application of fertilisers etc. Tea production has normally a gestation period of 4-5 years. Tea bush starts yielding from 4th to 5th years of the date of plantation. Taking cognizance of gestation period and occurrence of no abnormal year, investment figures of four years from 1994 to 1998, as available, were collected. Data incorporated in the test pertain to 24 units (2 each from well-performing and below-average category of gardens, and 10 each from average-performing and sick categories of gardens). The name of the estates have been kept confidential and instead some codes been used.

The Table 5.15 presents data relating to investment and production for 24 gardens, 10 each from 2nd and sick category, and 2 each from 1st and 3rd category. In order to study the impact of

Table 5.15: The Investment Made in Different Groups of Estates During 1994-1998 and Effect on Production

Sl.No	*Code name of gardens in different groups 1994-1998 (Rs.)*	*Average annual investment during*	*Annual investment per hectare (Rs.)*	*Production per hectare in 1998 (kg)*
1.	SG1	150411	3760	443
2.	SG8	760277	2725	1167
3.	SG10	255914	3130	371
4.	SG14	2425720	11178	1105
5.	SG15	6296	141	204
6.	SG20	17694	1179	500
7.	SG22	3300	103	250
8.	SG25	149194	2869	711
9.	SG26	629809	5292	905
10.	SG28	17554	399	875
11.	A1	2797585	10970	2741
12.	A2	6475872	16952	3151
13.	B1	2587012	8354	906
14.	B2	861994	11972	914
15.	B3	2159345	9188	2067
16.	B4	1162508	4687	1028
17.	B5	1998568	8504	2067
18.	B6	1332568	5330	1148
19.	B7	419108	1922	963
20.	B8	5388907	15943	1467
21.	B9	18345935	27381	2345
22.	B10	5322636	10929	1808
23.	C1	1394660	4265	810
24.	C2	2729507	3673	889

Source : Individual survey by the researcher

SG : Sick gardens, A : Well-performing gardens, B : Average-performing gardens, C: Below-average performing gardens annual investment per hectare (X) on productivity (Y) we have estimated regression of Y on X and tested its parameters as follows:

$$Y_i = 564.24+0.0895X_i$$

Further, we have taken,

the Null Hypothesis,

H_0 = Variables are independent (i.e., b=0.0895, is not significant)

t-test for studying relationship between the two variables gives us the following results.

The calculated value of 't' which is 5.19 is much higher than the table value with 23 d.f., hence, the null hypothesis that variables are not related is rejected at 5% level of significance (Annexure 4). Also a significant positive value of b is sufficient ground to conclude that amount of investment is an important determinant of productivity of tea estates. Thus, we can conclude from these results that if the provision of adequate finance is made for the sick gardens then there is high chance of improving the average productivity and that could help to minimise the magnitude of the problem of sickness. The above finding proves that "provision of adequate finance from public and/or bodies for the revival of sick units ensure solution of 'industrial sickness'."

Heterogeneity of Causal Factors

An indepth study of all the 28 sick tea estates of Barak Valley reveals that along with managerial and financial factors, the sick tea gardens are affected by some other factors which are heterogeneous in nature such as change of ownership, court case, encroachment, over staff etc. (Table 4.16).

It has been observed that major cause of sickness along with concomitant factors is financial in 12 gardens, mismanagement in 8 gardens, court cases in 5 gardens, encroachment in one garden, excess staff and reluctancy to revive in two other gardens. Out of these 28 gardens only 10 gardens have their own factories. Absence of own factory leaves the gardens with weak bargaining power in the leaf market as they cannot produce made tea. For selling their leaves they depend always on other gardens having factories and hence get exploited by the middlemen and gardens having factories.

Table 5.16: Analysis of Sick Gardens

Name of the gardens	*Own factory (Fa)*	*Finance (Fi)*	*Other problems*
SG1	Fa	Fi	
SG2	Fa		Unwilling to revive and invest
SG3	Fa		- do -
SG4		Fi	Ownership changed
SG5			Court case
SG6		Fi	Ownership change
SG7			Court case
SG8			Court case (family dispute)
SG9	Fa		Court case
SG10	Fa	Fi,	cleared liability
SG11		Fi	Ownership changed
SG12		Fi	Mismanagement
SG13	Fa	Fi	Mismanagement
SG14		Fi	Ownership changed, and encroachment problems
SG15			- do -
SG16	Fa		- do -
SG17			Mismanagement
SG18	Fa		- do -
SG19			- do -
SG20			- do -
SG21	Fa	Fi	Capital withdrawn
SG22			Mismanagement
SG23		Fi	
SG24			Court case
SG25	Fa		Encroachment
SG26		Fi	
SG27		Fi	Mismanagement
SG28			Excess staff

Source : Individual survey by the researcher

Majority of the sick gardens are proprietary gardens. When the original proprietor dies, then the ownership is passed on to persons as per the provision of law of inheritance. In a number of cases it has been observed that person/s on whom ownership is shifted, are settled in distant places or engaged in other activities. Such co-owners hardly take any interest on the development of the gardens but only remain interested to get their equal share from profit. Tea industry being completely nature-based industry remains at the mercy of weather. Two consecutive bad weather can easily throw an average garden into sickness. If at such time, the emergency fund remains weak and the owners do not provide sufficient financial support, the garden falls in the grip of sickness. The person managing such garden often finds it difficult to arrange fund by taking loan because, the precondition of loan i.e., mortgage of land, does not become feasible as other co-owners away from the field may not agree to do so.

Another aspect worth mention is the judicial system. In India, any appeal by any co-owner may get status-quo order by the court on the garden. This restricts the management from taking steps like extension, re-plantation or any other, which may be vital for the garden's general health. In fact, though for some gardens we have cited less investment as the cause of sickness, but this factor is originally the fall out of court cases or/and due to inheritance of ownership.

A tea garden should have a continuous process of development, any disturbance or uncertainty for some period of time gives rise to problems of various nature. One such problem, causing sickness in a garden in Barak Valley and creating a major obstacle on the way of its revival effort by its new sound proprietor a couple of years back, is encroachment of land. People from around that garden taking advantage of the inaction of the earlier management and transition period of the ownership of this garden, encroached the garden area in large scale. Later the new owner by applying his strong influence, which he commands in this valley, made the garden encroachment free. But every management may not always have this advantage and ultimately the garden suffers if the civil administration does not come forward..

Entrepreneurs' Views on Sickness

Let us have the views of the owners of sick gardens on the problems of sickness and their revival. In this context, personal interviews of three owners (termed A, B and C as they do not want to reveal their identity) are presented below :

Garden A

Statement of the garden owner who purchased a sick garden and succeed to revive it: "This garden was purchased in 1971 in sick condition. The earlier management was not very serious and the garden was encroached upon by the outsiders and got involved in as many as 150 no. of court cases. Due to these reasons the present management found great difficulties in evicting the encroachers."

Q. : What are the problems you came across in the way of revival of your garden?

Owner : Land ceiling act comes in the way of expansion of this garden. Supply of tea labourers is also saturating.. Capital from government and public sector institutions can not be completely relied upon as this involves a lengthy and complicated process. High cost of production due to high rate of agricultural tax imposed by the government. There is too much bureaucratic control over the production process. The garden had to complete various formalities with various departments leading to increased in cost of production.Transportation poses another big problem mainly, due to inadequate and ill-maintained roads. This garden is 69 km away from Silchar but takes 4 hours to reach there."

Q. : Why the 'Cachar Tea' has the stigma of poor quality?

Owner : "For average gardens in this valley the only source of R&D is TRA (Tea Research Association) which is far from satisfactory. R&D can be carried out by the gardens maintained by rich owners individually but an average tea garden can hardly do so."

Garden B

Q. : Your garden is sick. Why don't you make effort to revive your garden? What are the major problems you face in order to revive your garden?

Owner : The solution in curing sickness of my garden lies with large amount of investment. Bank loan involves high rate of interest. It requires a lengthy, complicated process with uneasy terms and conditions. Even to take loan from Tea Board, some pre-conditions are to be fulfilled. This involves large amount of initial expenditures. Due to this risk, the entrepreneur hesitates to take loan as tea industry falls prey to bad weather very often. If bad weather appears during sickness/expansionary stage, the owner becomes bankrupt. There are instances of such type of misfortune to some entrepreneurs in this valley in recent past. Even if the weak garden owner desires to take loan, he does not find it very easy to get the same. Bank loans are easily mobilised by the rich garden owners whose head offices are located in Calcutta. The decision regarding the loan of larger amounts are taken in the regional offices of banks, generally located in Calcutta. So, the rich tea gardens by maintaining liaison through their head offices in Calcutta with the banks can easily get the loan sanctioned. For weak gardens frequent visit to Calcutta and stay is not always affordable.

Garden C

Q. : What is the major cause of sickness of your garden?

Owner : By the law of inheritance, after the death of the original owner, the ownership shifted to next kin, the female members were away from the garden after marriage and the male partners except one were also in other places for higher study. During this period the garden was totally mismanaged and investment was insufficient. Recently this garden is reviving as quite large amount of capital has been invested, by taking loan from private sources. This has been possible as one co-owner after acquiring management qualification came back and took charge of this garden. Absence of own factory poses another problem to garden reducing its profitability. The garden has to sell green leaf to other rich gardens, generally via agent (middlemen) and there is large practice of advance sale. In such process a major portion of profits are eaten up by middlemen leaving very less amount for the original producer. Supply of labour has also been felt to be saturated. We are actually in receivers' end in the auction market, it is actually the purchasers' market. Deforestation causes serious threat to garden. Deforestation causes water logging in the planted area, causing damages to the tea bushes.

Results Obtained

The interview of owners reveal that the factors responsible for continuation of industrial sickness of the tea estates of Barak Valley are heterogeneous in nature. The major causes highlighted by them may be summarised as below:

1. Land Ceiling Act stands in the way of area expansion of the tea estates.
2. Inelastic labour supply limits the expansion of scale of production.
3. Stigma of 'Cachar Tea' (poor quality) deprives the tea of Barak Valley of their proper price.
4. Tea Auction Market through which tea is sold, is in reality, a buyer's market. The sellers always remain on the receiving end. An amount of 'monopsony' prevails in the Auction Centres.
5. Cost of production of tea in Barak Valley is very high. This is mainly due to high agricultural income tax and too much bureaucratic control over the production process. High cost of production and low price realisation reduce the margin of profit and thus, the capacity of ploughing back of capital in the gardens.
6. The facilities of institutional finance is mainly enjoyed by the corporate owners of tea estates. To get long term loans, the garden owners are needed to maintain liaison with the regional offices of

the financial institutions mostly located in Calcutta. The marginal garden owners could not afford such activities whereas the corporate owners of gardens could easily do so through their head offices (mostly) in Calcutta.

7. Investment in marginal gardens through institutional finance is very risky. This is so because the interest involvement with loan is very high, thus, puts a big burden of installment payment at regular interval. If the loanee entrepreneur faces unfavourable climate, any further loans drives the tea estates from bad to worse situation.

8. Deforestation which is responsible for occurrence of flood, causes damage to crops in some gardens of Barak Valley.

9. TRA (Tea Research Association) is the only source of R&D mainly to the weak gardens as they are incapable of maintaining their own R&D. The present functioning of TRA in Barak Valley is far from satisfactory.

The above views of the garden owners have been cross- examined from alternative sources. Except the following few points all others have been found to be quite valid in Barak Valley.

Regarding inelastic labour supply a trade union leader, in his interview, voiced a different opinion. According to him, inelasticity of labour supply is not due to labour supply saturation, it is rather other way round. Some garden owners offer such terms and conditions in their gardens that are not acceptable and hence, labourers do not offer themselves for employment in those gardens. This means that the labour supply is not actually inelastic for higher wages and other facilities. The view of the trade union leader is much realistic in view of the dismal employment situation prevailing in the tea garden population of Barak Valley.

The matter of high cost of production mentioned by the interviewed garden owners does not have much evidence. The analysis of cost of production of tea in this valley in Chapter 3, rather shows that it is relatively lower in Barak Valley when compared with Brahmaputra Valley and other parts of India.

The argument of risk factor involved in the institutional finance in tea industry is not quite convincing, it rather smacks of pessimism.

Risk is an undetachable component of every business. More efficient an entrepreneur is, more capable he is in minimising the risk.

This study in this chapter has applied various techniques to find out the causal factors of sickness in the tea estates of Barak Valley. These various techniques of investigation have unearthed a number of causal factors. All these factors invite sincere attention of the concerned authorities for their redressal in order to make Barak Valley a sickness-free tea zone.

6

Benefits from the Revival of Sick Units

In view of the seriously adverse impact of industrial sickness on the economy and on the society, as discussed in the chapter 5, often a straight solution of 'winding up' of the unit could be offered. In this regard, the practices in some developed countries are also cited. But it has been mentioned in earlier chapters that ground realities in those countries and in India are not the same. India is a capital-scarce and labour-abundant country. Moreover, shifting of sick industrial units, employment and rehabilitation in India is not that easy as in other developed countries like United Kingdom. Indian condition suits more to the effort of revival of sick units until it reaches the point of non-reversal, and this may be more beneficial for the economy than the other course of actions. In this chapter an attempt has been made to point out various probable benefits that may come out from the revival of the sick tea estates in Barak Valley. The benefits may be of wide range with far-reaching linkages. But it has not been possible to cover all such aspects. A simple method of analysis has been adopted in the present chapter to highlight the probable changes in the quantity of output, employment and direct income generation.

Favourable Impact on Production and Its Spread Effect

The sick gardens in Barak Valley are characterised by very low average productivity per hectare. The average productivity calculated from the information provided in the Table 7.1 for sick tea gardens of Barak Valley is as low as 652 kg per hectare which varies from one sick garden to another to a large extent. The minimum average productivity is worked out to be as low as 2.6 kg/hec as against the maximum average productivity of 866.97 kg/hec. For this low productivity the sickness only should be blamed because gardens like Arcuttipore, Combergram, Komber, Larsing, Daloo and Dewan which are economically sound in Barak Valley have reached the figures of 2741 kg, 2423 kg, 2596 kg, 2685 kg, 3134 kg, 2610 kg respectively as average productivity per hectare. The garden Rosekandi was in a very bad condition with a very low average productivity of 895 kg per hectare in 1985 and but by its sincere effort it has been able to improve its condition and now it is a successful garden. Its average productivity now has been raised to 2009 kg/hec. During the same period with a marginally increased area this garden became successful in increasing its total production from 433,440 kg to 1,125,000 kg, showing an additional production of 691,560 kg (Tea Board of India, Silchar). So, the sick gardens if revived, can reach to the average productivity level of the others (non-sick gardens) consequently there could be a significant increase in the total production of tea in Barak Valley, making strong positive impact on employment, income generation and on the whole economy. In order to assess the benefits from the revival of sick gardens it has been assumed that if revived, the sick gardens can produce at a average rate at which other non-sick gardens were producing as in 1998 (which has been calculated to a level at 2272 kg per hectare). Now, supposing that the revived sick gardens will produce at 2272 kg/hec, expected gross production from each sick garden has been calculated and the difference between the actual and expected gross production has been estimated and shown in the Table 7.1 as the measure of benefit from the revival of sick gardens.

The net benefit in production expected after the revival of the sick gardens may be of the tune of 3320.55 thousand kg. This increase in production will certainly bring a significant change in the whole tea industry of Barak Valley. This additional production when sold (at the average price prevailing in 1998), will provide the excess income to each sick garden as shown in table 7.1 totalling a sum of Rs. 22.57 crores. Tea industry has strong forward and backward linkages.

Table 6.1: Expected Benefits from the Revival of Sick Gardens in Terms of Production and Income

Sl. No.	*Code name of the garden*	*Present*			*Expected production after revival (kg)*	*Net gain after revival (kg)*	*Addl. Income generation at price Rs.68/-*
		area under production (hec)	*Production (kg)*	*Average productivity (kg/hec)*			
1.	SG 1	287	334776	1166	652064	317288	21575584
2.	SG2	430	318143	739.86	976960	658817	44799556
3.	SG3	98	19342	197.36	222656	203314	13825352
4.	SG4	377	326850	866.97	856544	529694	36019192
5.	SG5	327	189332	579	742944	553612	37645616
6.	SG6	125	21434	171.47	284000	262566	17854488
7.	SG7	155	80482	519.23	352160	271678	18474104
8.	SG8	32	8000	250	72704	64704	4399872
9.	SG9	250	189750	759	568000	378250	27721000
10.	SG10	227.88	151364	664	518016	366652	24932336
11.	SG11	52	37224	716	118144	80920	5502560
12.	SG12	153	73788	482	347616	273828	18620304
13.	SG13	238	186773	785	540736	353963	24069484
14.	SG14	135	351	2.60	306720	306369	20833092
15.	SG15	308	31416	102	699776	668360	45448480
16.	SG16	571	487225	853	1297312	810087	55085916
17.	SG17	69858	684747	9.80	1585856	901109	61275412
18.	SG18	500	178463	356.92	1136000	957537	65112516
19.	SG19	325	152009	467.72	738400	586391	39874588
20.	SG20	818	628553	768	1858496	1229943	83636124
21.	SG21	43	16106	374.56	97696	81590	5548120
22.	SG22	49	663	13.53	111328	110665	7525220
23.	SG23	NA	NA				
24.	SG24	73	29193	400	165856	13663	929084

25.	SG25	145	44829	309	329440	284611	19353548
26.	SG26	24	4888	203.66	54528	49640	3375520
27.	SG27	159	119216	750	361248	242032	16458176
28.	SG28	44	16673	378.90	99968	83295	5664060
	Total	6643	4331590	652	1011040	3320550	225797400

Source: Tea Board of India, Silchar & Individual survey by the researcher.

This industry indirectly helps development of bamboo and cane industry, production of jute bags for processed tea, transport sector, the sale of various consumer items supplied to garden labourers like shoe, blanket, torch-light etc. The generation of additional income besides giving a fillip to the above sectors will contribute large amount to government exchequer in the form of agricultural income tax, sales tax, excise duty and other cess. The financial resources locked up in the sick gardens will get their proper utilisation and return back to the lender institutions from additional income. Expenditure on the production of each additional kg of tea will give additional income to various sectors of the economy having multiplier effect.

Favourable Impacts on Employment and Land Utilisation

In studying the likely effect on employment from the revival of sick gardens, it has been observed that the employment ratio (labour per hectare) in sick and sound gardens shows much divergence. When the corresponding ratio in sick gardens in 1998 was 1.78 it was 2.54 in non-sick gardens (Tea Board of India, Silchar). The average employment ratio representing both sick and non-sick gardens is estimated to be 2.24 in Barak Valley. If the ratio changes from 1.78 to 2.24 after revival there would be some considerable additional employment. One thing that should not be left from discussion is the case of temporary labour. The employment scenario that we have considered so far is that of permanent labourers, whose figures are actually supplied by tea gardens and available in Provident Fund list. It is very difficult to get the exact picture of temporary labourers in each garden because of their temporary nature of job. But the incidence of sickness first fall on the temporary labourers and the benefit of revival also are first enjoyed by the temporary labourers. The ratio of temporary labourer to total adult employment was 21.19% in 1997 (Mazumdar, ed., 2001). Another aspect that deserves mention here is that the present figure of employment per hectare of land in Barak Valley seems to be too low at 2.24 when it is 2.56 in Brahmaputra Valley beside the fact that labour productivity in Barak Valley is 735 (kg/labour) higher than the Brahmaputra Valley at 733 (kg/labour).

Some of the sick gardens are closed and some are producing much below their capacity. Once revived the development process will get momentum and the expansion of cultivation which was stagnant during sickness will restart. Large number of sick tea estates have huge areas available for extension. If these areas are brought under cultivation with the income earned after revival there would be enormous increase in production, income and employment. The areas available for extension and the resultant employment generation in the sick gardens for which information are available in 1995, are given Table 7.2.

Table 6.2: Area Extension and Employment Generation from Revival of Sick Gardens

Sl. No.	*Code name of the sick gardens*	*Area available for extension (hec)*	*Additional employment*
1.	SG1	300.00	672
2.	SG2	7.66	17
3.	SG4	4.05	9
4.	SG5	200.00	448
5.	SG6	260.65	584
6.	SG9	100.00	224
7.	SG16	49.80	112
8.	SG17	85.00	179
9.	SG19	103.49	232
10.	SG23	43.20	97
11.	SG25	342.85	768
12.	SG26	30.00	67
13.	SG27	121.46	272
14.	SG28	350.00	784
	Total	1998.16	4465

Source: Tea Board of India Individual survey by the researcher

Information available from 14 sick gardens show that 1998.16 hectares of land areas suitable for cultivation but are remaining unutilised due to paucity of fund. Bringing this vast area under tea crop these tea gardens will bring wide range of benefits to the economy from increase in production, income and employment. Taking 2.24 as standard employment-land ratio, the likely additional employment could be to the tune of 4465 persons with its linkage effect in Barak Valley.

Environmental Impact and Sustainable Development

The aspect of environment is fast attracting the attention of intelligentsia over the world. Mere economic development is no longer the sole objective of the economy in the world. In the present milieu the priority is on 'sustainable development' in order to meet both current and future human needs and aspirations.

Sustainable development embraces three basic concepts – the economic, the social and environmental. The economic component of sustainability requires that societies pursue economic growth paths that generate an increase in true income, that lead to long term impoverishment. Social dimension of sustainable development is built on the premises that over a long period, wealth resources and opportunity must be shared in a manner that all citizens have access to minimum standards of security, human rights and social benefits such as food, health, education, shelter and opportunities for self-development. The environmental dimension of sustainable development is predicated on maintaining the long term integrity and therefore, the productivity of the plant's life-support system and environmental infrastructure.

In the process of development utmost importance should be laid on such activities which are more environment friendly. The environmental degradation has serious adverse effect on the economy. One probable consequence of global warming explains the seriousness of the problem "a one meter rise in sea level due to global warming, if it were to happen today, would displace 7 million people in India and submerge 35% of the land in Bangladesh (Parikh 2000).

Some recent studies have also found a very close link between environmental degradation and poverty. The World Development

Report, 1992 (p. 7), notes that the poor are both victims and agents of environmental damage'. Tea industry has a great role in preserving and developing a good environment. Tea industry with its tea bushes and big trees for shades to bushes at regular distance provide green cover on land and contribute to afforestation. Tea is mainly cultivated on '*tillahs*' and hill slopes and it, thus, prevents soil erosion. The present researcher observed that sickness in tea estates gradually lead to depletion of big trees and tea bushes, which in extreme circumstances are used as last resort to earn some income. As command and control method has lost its significance in recent times in preserving environment giving place to market linked technique, the revival of the sick gardens would go a long way in solving various economic problems faced by the people and marking the region environmentally enriched.

7

Conclusion and Suggestions

The concern of the present study has been the nature and consequences of the sickness of tea plantation units in Barak Valley. This concern for the major organised sector of the valley has found expression in adopting the objectives of our investigation. First, we have attempted to identify the factors contributing to sickness in tea gardens. Here the management aspect has drawn our main attention. Secondly, an assessment of impact of industrial sickness on the economy of Barak Valley has been attempted. Thirdly, we have also shown the likely benefits that may be derived from revival of sick gardens. Lastly, in the light of our findings we propose to offer suggestions in this chapter. Let us first make a summary of findings achieved so far and have a look at the results of testing of hypothesis.

Summary of Findings

In the review of existing literature on industrial sickness it has been found that though there are several studies on 'industrial sickness' in general, but most of the studies are based on corporate sectors or public sector undertakings. The analysis of causal factors were mainly based on financial ratios available in the well maintained Balance sheets. But the tea industry being agro-based industry requires a special technique for study its sickness. Recognising such special feature of tea industry, the Government of India has also adopted a special method to define sickness in tea industry. In fact, no indepth and precise study has been made so far to identify the various visible and invisible causes of sickness in tea industry.

The study of the performance of tea industry in Barak Valley during the pre and Post-Independence period gives at a gloomy picture when compared with Brahmaputra Valley and India. The performance of Barak Valley was rather opposite in some period during the early days of tea plantation in Assam. At some point of time the tea industry of Barak Valley earned the distinction of the producer of largest quantity and of finest variety, recognised in world market, among the tae producing districts of Assam. The only advantage of tea cultivation in Barak Valley is the low cost of production. But this advantage seldom yields any benefit to the producer due to low price realisation.

The investigation into the causes of sickness in the tea estates of Barak Valley finds 'mismanagement' and 'less investment' as the two principal factors. These two factors happen to be the main causes of sickness in 70% of the sick gardens in Barak Valley. Other causal factors detected in this study are frequent change of ownership, insufficient credit, and complicated credit facility, poor R&D activities, lengthy disposal of court cases, encroachment problem and deforestation.

The analysis of impact of 'industrial sickness' reveals serious socioeconomic consequences in the economy. It leads to large scale loss of employment, production and blockage of scarce resources of the country. The total bank credit blocked up in 'sick industrial units' in India till 31st March 1998 was Rs. 15,682 crores. The effect of sickness of tea industry on the economy of Barak Valley has been found to be very serious as it is the major industry to provide employment and generate income in this valley.

The role of government institutions in preventing and curing 'industrial sickness' in Barak Valley has been found to be very demoralising. The government institutions have so far remained less responsive to this serious problem. It is worth mentioning that almost all the gardens under the management of government institutions in Barak Valley are either 'sick' or 'weak'.

The projection of likely benefits from the revival of 'sick' tea units in Barak Valley has been found to be very lucrative and motivating. The projected benefits from the revival of 'sick gardens' are additional production to the extent of 33 lakh kg, additional income of Rs. 22

crores and 4465 number of additional employment with a wide range of linkage effect.

While undertaking study and analysing the data, the hypotheses set in the introduction chapter are tested and proved to be true. The first hypothesis of this study "Scientific management plays vital role for healthy existence of business enterprises in the competitive market" has been found to be valid in the test. The test reveals that gardens with management of different levels of efficiency produce with different level of average productivity. Higher level of managerial efficiency results in higher average productivity and vice-versa. Low productivity makes cost of production high which reduces the competitive strength of the enterprise in the market.

The test of our second hypothesis, "Impact of sickness on production, employment and competitive strength of the enterprise in the market proves serious" has been completely dealt with in chapter five. This chapter reveals the extent of loss in production, income generation at both macro and micro level. The reduction in the competitive strength of the enterprise due to sickness has found to be valid in the case studies of some gardens.

In the testing of our third hypothesis, "Provision of adequate finance from public bodies for the revival of sick units ensure solution of industrial sickness", it has been found that investment has a strong influence on productivity in the tea estates of Barak Valley. The estates which have made higher investment on field activities have become successful in raising their average productivity per hectare in gardens.

Suggestions

The importance of tea industry in the economy of Barak Valley as well as in India has been well documented in the present study. It is one of the major labour-intensive industries employing male and female workers in equal ratio besides its other roles as foreign currency earner, great contributor to state and central governments exchequer, environment protector and promoter of other ancillary industries. Further, it follows from the other chapter that though tea industry in Barak Valley is in a bad shape with a very low average yield and large number of sick gardens, it was not so in the beginning during mid-nineteenth century. In some years tea of Barak Valley exhibited better performance than Brahmaputra Valley both in quantitative and qualitative terms. So it would not be proper to blame only nature for the present fate of this valley's tea industry. If the main factors detected so far responsible for industrial sickness in tea industry of Barak Valley are properly addressed by finding out suitable means, certainly this industry will be able to regain its lost glory. Accordingly the following suggestions are proposed:

1. Restriction on Unhealthy Change of Ownership and Management of Gardens

Tea industry being an agro-based industry with a long gestation period deserves a special type of care. Any development plan for the revival of sick garden is a long and continuous process. Any disruption in the process would result in complete failure. A tea plant after its plantation takes around five years to yield production and during this period the plant needs continuous nourishment. Any gap in this process will result in drying up of the plant. Even the grown up bushes need regular treatment. Thus, frequent changes of ownership/management is counterproductive to the health of tea estates. Change in ownership/management often results in discontinuation of earlier pans and programmes because the new owner/management may have his own perception and motive. The government must act as the watchdog and exercise some control over the frequent change in ownership and transfer of ownership to inept hand. The government also should put its own house in order. Instances are plenty in Barak Valley that for protect some weak gardens were brought under the ownership of government agencies and they became sick. In one sick garden of this valley which was under direct control of the Deputy Commissioner of the concerned district, the officer in charge has been subject to frequent change. So when one officer who takes in hand some development programmes is transferred and a new person is assigned the job may not like the programmes taken by his predecessor. A development programme once taken, if not continued will affect the whole production process of tea and cause unnecessary erosion of fund. The continuity is a vital factor so far as ownership and management are concerned.

2. Government Monitoring of Development Activities

Management which has been found in this study as the major factor behind industrial sickness needs qualitative improvement. Scientific management should replace traditional family based management. Majority of the gardens in Barak Valley became sick under proprietary ownership. What has been observed that a garden after being inherited by the young members of the family are looked after by only one or two members, the rest remain aloof or outstationed but reaping the benefit of their share. Gardens are considered only as a source of income but the aspects of its maintenance, nourishment etc. are completely ignored. Such practice causes irreparable damage to the garden. In one such garden in this valley, even the shade trees were felled and sold to earn income. Such type of problems are most common in proprietary and Pvt. Ltd. types of ownership. Tea estates are often purchased for speculative purposes to earn quick profits. This means the tea gardens are treated not as productive ventures but as mines from which one may attempt to extract as much as possible without caring for the long-term consequences. Due to this reason the valley had some uneconomic gardens even during the British period, and this problem still remain unattended. As the sickness of tea estates does not affect the owner only it affects the whole economy and causes loss of nation's resource, the Government should not remain a silent spectator. The Government may engage some supervising authority with power to take action over all gardens who will investigate the development activities like manuring, infilling, rejuvenation etc. Lack of such activities have left this valley with large number of uneconomic tea bushes and high vacancy ratio. If the above method is adopted then the gardens would get proper attention before they become sick.

3. Qualitative Improvement of Management

In order to make qualitative improvement of the management the following steps are suggested:

i) Introduction of scientific management in place of century old traditional family based management.

ii) Some minimum technical and managerial qualification requirement for persons in management.

iii) Membership of TRA (Tea Research Association) must be made compulsory. It has been found in course of study that 50% of surveyed gardens are not members of TRA.

iv) It has been alleged by some garden owners that TRA in Barak Valley is almost defunct. So, government should take necessary steps to re-activate the TRA so that it can contribute technical advancement of tea cultivation.

v) It has been observed a some public limited and private limited gardens that too much centralisation of power handicaps the local management to act on time and take necessary steps. Tea industry being agro-based may at any time require instant action. In this context some decentralisation of power is desired.

4. Common Tea Processing Units

Availability of own factory is a bare necessity for gardens to improve the quality of their tea and to get the proper price of products. But the investigation of all the 28 sick gardens reveals that 64% sick gardens in Barak valley do not have their own factory. Here it appears that a satisfactory solution of the problems connected with the manufacture of tea in the sick estates would pose even greater difficulties than those concerning plantation. It is not economically viable for a garden producing a small quality of green leaf to have a factory that has to run at only a fraction of its capacity. One solution to this problem is to have a common factory for some adjacent gardens. Special precautions here have to be taken to ensure that the leaf does not lose its freshness before it reaches the factory to start the operation of withering, otherwise, the quality of made tea is adversely affected.

5. Easy Finance

The process of safeguarding the gardens from becoming sick or revival from sickness involves some crucial activities like regular infilling, rejuvenation and proper manuring of the tea bushes, construction of factory, extension cultivation etc. But these activities can hardly be taken up if the weak gardens are not provided with adequate finance. Though there are a number of institutions to provide credit to tea estates credit flow is not materialised in the case of weak and sick tea estates. A major difficulty in the way of a garden obtaining term credit is its inability to provide the type of security acceptable to the lending institution. The estate or garden property is itself the principal security that can be offered for this purpose. However, the property is also in a number of cases charged as collateral security for working capital finance. Under the existing conditions where the garden has to approach a term lending institution for long term finance and commercial banks for working capital, this entails a conflict of interest. The term lending institution seeks a first charge on the property but often finds it difficult to obtain this because of the reported reluctance of the commercial banks to release its charge on the same held as collateral.

In order to overcome the above mentioned problem what is suggested is that, if both working capital and term finance need are channelised through a single agency it would be able to undertake the assessment of the overall financial requirements, work out the tenure of term loans, lay down the criteria for sharing the security, follow up the use of funds and generally keep in touch with the borrowing units. This however, would not mean that the agency envisaged should take on itself the entire financial burden. The agency would seek to apportion the required credit among the various institutions, thus, drawing on their resources and specialised know-how and generally act as sponsoring agent or consortium leader. Tea Board, which though not primarily a financial institution, has until now been the main source of development finance for the industry and it should be in the consortium of credit institutions.

The gardens in need of urgent credit report of unusual delay in loan sanction and involvement of avoidable expenditure, which got mentioned in Chapter 4. To avoid such obstacles, some decentralisation in the functioning of Tea Board and other financial institutions are suggested. The district level branches need to be entrusted with more powers to sanction loans. The local garden owners cannot always afford to visit Calcutta frequently or stay there for a long duration in order to get their loan sanctioned early. Moreover, such expenditure only unnecessarily erode the limited funds.

6. Tea Industry in 'Priority Sector'

The tea industry by virtue of its importance as a foreign exchange earner and provider of huge employment deserves a recognition of 'priority sector'. So whether or not this de facto situation is given de jure recognition, it is expected that financial institutions would give high priority to tea industry while formulating policies.

7. Utilisation of Unused Area

In view of the existence of huge amount of unutilised area within the total grant area, it is suggested that the effort should be made to use them for some other commercial purposes. This will help in the generation of fund within the garden itself which could be used for development of tea cultivation.

8. Early Disposal of Court Cases

Lengthy disposal of court cases of some tea estates poses a great problem for the entrepreneur to initiate any development programme. Sometimes judiciary directs the management not to make any major decision till the case is disposed. During this period the owner can't take loan even in emergency situations due to his inability to mortgage the document of the estate. The absence of proper care of the tea bushes for some period causes irreparable damage to the estates aggravating sickness. Recently, the government has initiated some reform in the judicial process. There is now some special provision for early disposal of court cases in some areas. Tea industry, being a special type industry deserves some special attention from judiciary for quick settlement of court cases particularly, ownership disputes.

Conclusion

It cannot be overemphasised that apart from its national importance tea plantation industry occupies the central position in the organised economic activities of Barak Valley. In fact, revival of the sick plantation units is almost a life and death question of the economy of Barak Valley. This valley which is suffering from relative economic stagnation can rediscover its growth-booster only in the rejuvenated tea gardens. The present researcher was motivated to undertake the study out of this concern for the economy of Barak Valley and therefore, it is expected that the results of the study would attract the attention of the policy makers. It is also hoped that the authorities will adopt appropriate measures to remedy the problems in the light of the suggestions offered in the present study.

ANNEXURE-I

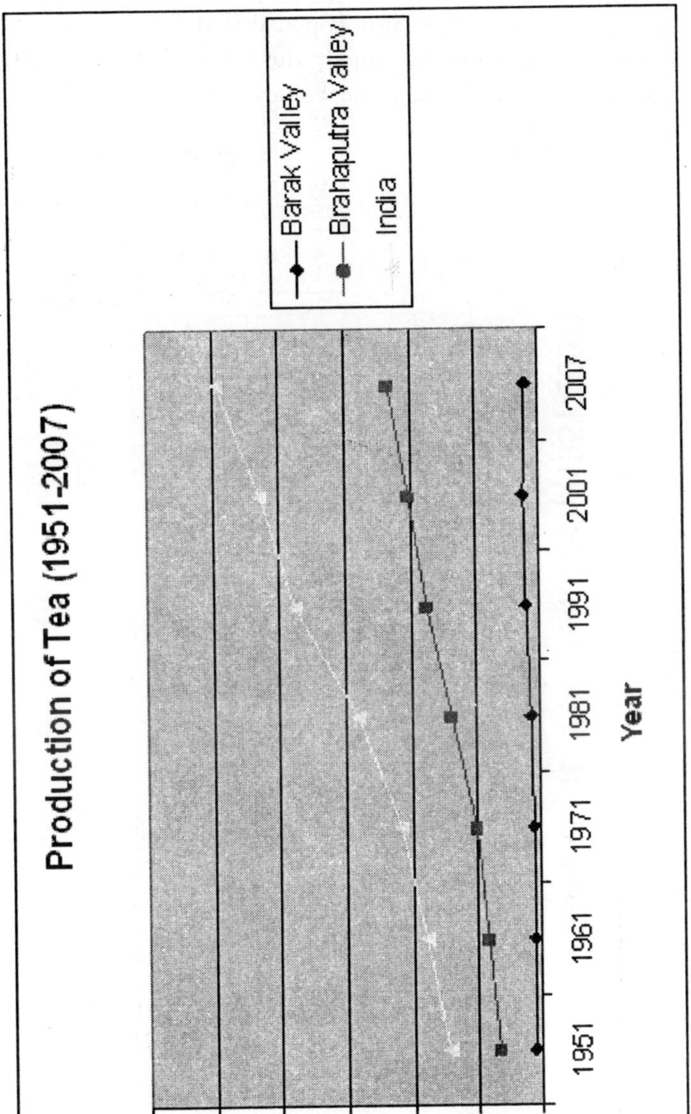
Production of Tea (1951-2007)
Barak Valley
Brahaputra Valley
India
Production ('000 kg)
1200
1000
800
600
400
200
0
1951
1961
1971
1981
1991
2001
2007
Year

ANNEXURE-II

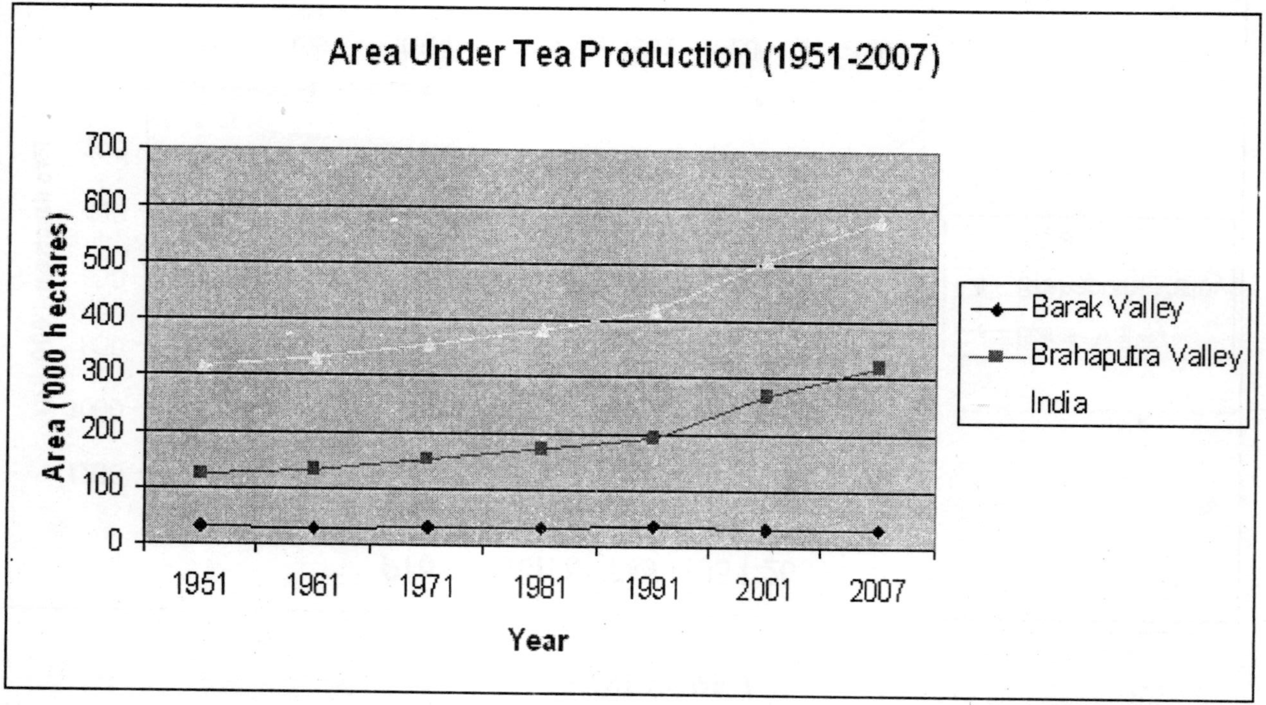
Area Under Tea Production (1951-2007)
700
600
500
400
300
200
100
0
Area ('000 hectares)
1951
1961
1971
1981
1991
2001
2007
Year
Barak Valley
Brahaputra Valley
India

Bibliography

Altman, E.I., Haldeman, R.G. and Narayan, P. (1980). 'Zeta Analysis : A New Model to Identify Bankruptcy Risk of Corporation', *Journal of Banking and Finance*, North Holland.

Altman, E.I. (1968). 'The Success of Business Failure Prediction Models: An International Surveym *Journal of Banking and Finance*, North Holland, Vol. 8, No. 2, June.

Awasti, R C. (1968). *Economics of Tea Industry*, United Publishers, Guwahati.

Banerjee, Bhabatosh (1992). "Rehabilitation of Sick Units: An Indian Experience," *Management Accountant*, Vol. 27, December.

Banerjee, M. (1970). *Business Administration – Principles and Technologies*, 3rd edition, Asian Publishing House, New Delhi.

Barah, B.C. and T. Chranjeevi (1991). 'Analysis of Area Decision in the Supply Response Model of India Tea', *Indian Journal of Agricultural Economics*, 46(4), October-December.

Bateman Merill J.(1965). 'Aggregate and Regional Supply functions for Ghanaian Cocoa – 1946-1963', *Journal of Farm Economics*, Vol. 43, No. 2, May.

Beaver, W. (1967). 'Financial Ratios as predictive of failure, in Empirical Research in Accounting', *Journal of Accounting Research*, January.

Bhattacharjee, J. (1977). *Cachar Under British Rule*, Radiant Publishers, New Delhi.

Bhattacharjee, S.K. (1989). *Achieving Managerial Excellence*, McMillan India.

Bhushan, Y.K. (1993). *Fundamentals of Business Organisation and Management*, Sultan Chand and Sons, New Delhi.

Bidani, S.N. and Mitra P.K. (1988). *Industrial Sickness - Identification and Rehabilitation*, Vision Books Pvt. Ltd., New Delhi.

Brech, E.F.L. (1965). *Principles and Practice of Management*, Longmans Green and Co. Ltd.

Cachar Plantation Committee Report (1950). Ministry of Labour, Government of India, New Delhi.

Chakraborty, S.K. and P.K. Sen (1980). *Industrial Sickness and Revival in India: Essays, Cases and Debates*, IIM, Calcutta.

Chatterjee, Haraprasad (1991). 'Industrial Sickness: Dimension, Roots and Orderly Revival', *Management Accountant*, 26(10), October.

Chiranjeevi, T. (1992). 'Indian Tea Industry', *Journal of Indian School of Political Economy*, 4(2), April-June.

Daga, N.K. (1985). 'Tea Industry: Problems and Prospects', *Capital*, 195(4812), 19 August.

Dasgupta, M. (1984). 'Sickness of Darjeeling Tea Industry', *North Bengal Economics*, Jan-March.

Dave, V. Nalini, (1987). *Industrial Sickness and Key Arrears of Management*, Deep and Deep Publications, New Delhi.

Directorate of Economics and Statistics, Government of Assam, Silchar.

Digest of Tea Statistics (1971-72). Tea Board of India.

Dutta, S.K. (1992). 'Indian Tea Industry: An Appraisal', *Management Accountant*, 27(3), March.

Economic Survey of India (1999-2000). Ministry of Finance, Government of India, New Delhi.

Elherington, Dam, M. and Foster (1993). 'China's Tea Industry at Crossroad on the Long March', *Singapore Economic Review*, 38(1), April.

Fisher, T. (Esq. AAGG) (1834). Letter to G S Gordon, Secretary, Committee for Tea Culture, London, dt. 25th March.

French, Ben C. and L Jim Mathews. (1971). 'A Study Response Model for Perennial Crops', *American Journal of Agricultural Economics*, August.

Fulmer, J.G. Jr. (1984). 'A Bankruptcy Classification Model for Small Firms', *Journal of Commercial Bank Lending*, Philadelphia, July.

Gadgil, P.G. and P.L. Gadgil (1985). *Industrial Economy of India*, Eurasia Publishing House (Pvt) Ltd., New Delhi.

Gaith, E. (1962). *The History of Assam*, Lawyers' Publications, Guwahati.

Gosh, B.C. (1972). 'Trends in Tea Industry During the First Twenty-five Years of Independence', *Economic Affairs*, 17(11), November.

Goswami Committee Report, (1993), Ministry of Finance, Government of India, New Delhi.

Griffith, P. (1967). *History of Indian Tea Industry*, Weidenfold and Nicolson, London.

Guha-Kasnobis Basudeb, (1995) *A Normative Analysis of the New Economic Policy of India*, University of Rochester.

Gupta, L.C. (1983). *Financial Ratios for Monitoring Corporate Sickness: Towards a More Systematic Approach*, Oxford University Press, Delhi.

Guthmann, H.G. (1978). *Analysis of Financial Statistics*, Prentice Hall of India, New Delhi.

Hampton, J.J. (1986). *Financial Decision Making: Concepts, Problems and Cases*, Prentice-Hall of India, New Delhi.

Handa, Rajiv (1992). 'Sickness in Industry: A Bankers Role', *Management Accountant*, 27(7), July.

India 2000, Ministry of Information and Broadcasting, Government of India.

Jayalakshmi, U. (1986). 'Industrial Sickness in India: Causes, Consequences and Policy Measures', *Southern Economist*, 24(19), 1 February.

Johnston, J. (1984). *Econometric Methods*, 3rd ed., McGraw-Hill International Book Company, Delhi.

Johri, C.K. (1992). *Industrialism and Employment Systems in India*, Oxford University Press, New Delhi.

Joshi, V.K. (1987). *Management of Industrial Sickness*, Kuber Associates and Publishers, Jaipur.

Kaveri, V.S. and S.P. Singh. (1976). 'Predicting Health of Borrowing Firms: Use of Technical Ratios', *Prajnan*, Bombay, July-September.

Khan, N.A. (1990). *Sickness in Industrial Units*, Anmol Publication, New Delhi.

Khanka, S.S. (1995). *Industrial Sickness in India*, Commonwealth Publisher, New Delhi.

Khanna, S.S. *et al.* (1990). 'Tea Production in India: Retrospect and Prospect', *Yojana*, 34(9), 16 May.

Kulkarni, P.V. (1988). *Business Finance: Principles and Problems*, Himalayan Publishing House, Bombay.

Lal, S. (1985). *How to Prevent Industrial Sickness: Symptoms and Rehabilitation*, Navrang Publishers and Booksellers, New Delhi.

Laycock, D.H. (1970). 'Two leaves and a Bud', Vol. 17, No. 4, December.

Lundy, J.L. (1968). *Effective Industrial Management*, Eurasia Publishing House Pvt. Ltd., New Delhi.

Marcelle Arak (1968). "The supply of Brazilian Coffee and the price responsiveness of Sao Paolo Coffee Growers," *Food Research Institute Studies*, No. 3, 1968, (PhD Thesis, MIT).

Mazumdar, A. (2001). "Tea Industry in Cachar: A Statistical Profile," *Centenary Souvenir (1901-2001)*. Surma Valley Branch Indian Association, Silchar.

Mehta, S.S. and Dinesh Harode (1999). 'Industrial Sickness and Workers', *EPW*, Dec 26, 1998-Jan 1, 1999.

Mishra, J.P. and A Sharma (1994). 'Revival of Tea Industry in Weak Tea States', *Yojana*, 38(23), 31 December.

Mishra, Sib Ranjan (1979). 'Relative Contribution of Different Components Towards Tea Production in North Bengal Tea Gardens', *Tea Association of India Newsletter*, 1979.

Mishra, Sib Ranjan. (1986). *Tea Industry in India*, Ashish Publishing House, New Delhi.

Mitra, Neelanjan (1991). 'Indian Tea Industry: Problems and Policies', *Economic and Political Weekly*, 26(48), 30 November.

Moitra, Neelanjana (1993). *Indian Tea Industry*, Anupama Publication, New Delhi.

Mukherjee, D. and P. Dey Sarkar. (1990). 'Tea Industry Needs Revamping', *Yojana*, May 16-31.

Mukherjee, Dhurati and Patatri De Sarkar (1990). 'Tea Industry Needs Revamping', *Yojana* 34(9), 16 May.

Nagaiya, D. (1991). *Industrial Sickness – A Health Monitoring Approach*, Discovery Pub. House, New Delhi.

NCAER (1961). *Economically Weak Tea Gardens in North East India.*

NCAER (1962) *Techno-Economic Survey of Assam.*

Pai, V.S. and Rajmani Aniebam (1991). 'Role of Tea Industry in North East India: A Strategy Analysis', *Journal of North East India Council*, 15(2), October.

Pande, K.M. and C.D. Bhattacharjee. 'Corporate Financial Strength, Application of MDA', *Jodhpur Management Journal*, vol. 3.

Parikh, K. Joti (2000). 'Inequality: A Root Cause of Climate Change', *IHDP Update*, November 3.

Paul, A.K. (1972). 'Tea Industry in Cachar', Ph.D. Thesis. (Gauhati University), unpublished.

Peters, Thomas J. and Robert H Waterman (1982). *In Search of Excellence*, Harper and Row Publishers, New York.

Raidwan, Ali (1977). 'Sri Lanka's Tea Industry: Succeeding in Global Market', World Bank, Washington DC.

Reddy, V.N. and Sharit K Bhowmic (1989). 'Small Growers and Cooperative Tea Factories in Nilgiris', *Economic and Political Weekly*, 24(39), 30 September.

Report of the Plantation Enquiry Commission (1956). Govt. of India, New Delhi.

Report of the Tea Finance Committee (1964). Government of India, New Delhi.

Report of the Working Group – 5 (1996). World Bank Assistance to Tea Industry in India, Ministry of Commerce, Government of India, New Delhi.

Report of the Working Group of Finance for Tea Industry (1972), Reserve Bank of India.

Report of the Working Group on Plantation Crops - Sub Group on Tea. (1964). Planning Commission, Government of India, New Delhi.

Report on Currency and Finance (1998), Reserve Bank of India, Bombay.

Report on Financial and Cost Survey of Tea Plantation and Industry, 1958-62, 1968, Tea Board of India.

Roy, Bedprakash Syam (1992), *Industrial Sickness*, Rupa Books Pvt. Ltd., Jaipur.

Sample Survey of Unemployment Situation of Tea Gardens of Assam (1958).

Sardar, A. (1991). 'Tea Industry : Ailment and Remedy', *Yojana*, 35(5), 16 March.

Sarkar, Gautam K. (1972). *The World Tea Economy,* Oxford University Press, Calcutta.

Sengupta, S.R. (1981). 'Raising Financing for Tea Industry: Constraints and Remedies', *Economic Times*, 12 February.

Sharma, Kailash Chandra. (1992). 'Tea production: Problems and Prospects', *Rural India*, 55(9), 15 August.

Sharma, L.V.N. and G.B. Rao. (1982). 'Financial Ratios as Predictors of Failure : A Nonvariate Approach', *Indian*, April-Jun.

Sharma, R.G. (1992). 'A Glimpse of Tea Industry in India', *Southern Economist*, 31(8), 15 August.

Sinha, Rathna (1988). 'Causes and Remedies of Industrial Sickness', *Management Accountant*, 23(4), April.

Srivastava, S.S. and R.A. Jadav. (1986). *Management and Monitoring of Industrial Sickness*, Concept Publishing Company, New Delhi.

Tea Board Manual Abstract: The Act – 1953 amended up to 4.6.1977.

Tea Statistics, (1995-96). Tea Board of India.

Techno-Economic Survey of Cachar Tea Industry (1982), Tea Board of India.

Trivedi, P.H. (1984). 'Industrial Rehabilitation with Special Reference to Assam', *Journal of NEC*, March-April, Vol. VI, No. 2.

Tsuruoka, Doug (1993). 'Brewed for Toollong: Malaysia's Tea Industry Struggles to Modernise', *Far Eastern Economic Review*, Vol. 5 & 6, May 20.

Index

□□□